The Spiritual Journey of
JOEL S. GOLDSMITH

The Spiritual Journey of

Lorraine Sinkler

JOEL S. GOLDSMITH
Modern Mystic

The Valor Foundation

Other books by Lorraine Sinkler include *SPIRITUAL ODYSSEY: The Unfoldment of a Soul* and *The Alchemy of Awareness*.

Designed by Dorothy Schmiderer

Library of Congress Cataloging in Publication Data

Sinkler, Lorraine.
  The spiritual journey of Joel S. Goldsmith.

  Includes bibliographical references.
    1. Goldsmith, Joel S   1892-1964.   2. New
Thought. I. Title.
BF648.G64S57   1973   289.9 [B]   72-13190
ISBN 0-9629119-2-5

 Contents

 Preface

The material for this book has been taken from many sources: the tape recordings of Joel Goldsmith's lectures and classes, letters written by him to me, conversations with him, and other unpublished material he gave me to use as I saw fit. Wherever possible, as indicated by the indented material, I have let him tell the story in his own words which have been taken directly from the above-mentioned sources. Because of this, practically every statement can be documented, and the accuracy of this work is thereby assured.

Beyond all that, however, is my personal recollection of him. I was privileged to have a close contact with Joel Goldsmith for fifteen years. For several of those fifteen years, as many as twenty-six weeks out of a year were spent in Hawaii, working with him from ten o'clock in the morning until eight or nine o'clock in the evening, and at one time I had the privilege of living in the Goldsmith home for three months. Day after day I found myself listening spellbound to Joel as he reeled off one fascinating story after another about his experiences. When I could no longer contain myself, I told him that I thought I should write down some of the things he was saying. This met with a quick response: "Yes, you must do that. In fact, you should carry a notebook with you wherever you go because one day you will have to write my story and that of The Infinite Way."

To aid in writing that story and in fulfilling what from that time on became a commitment, Joel sent me bundles of private papers he had accumulated over the years, some dating as far back as 1940, the first of which he sent in 1957 and the last in 1964, shortly before he left on his final trip to England. So I have a priceless treasure of little scribbled notes in his own handwriting, many of them on scraps of paper yellowed with age, a diary, and other bits of writing, including a skeleton outline of what he called his spiritual autobiography. All of this, plus an exchange of an average of from two to six letters a week from October, 1949, to May, 1964, made an indelible impression on me and gave me an unusual opportunity to observe at firsthand this remarkable man.

While every fact in this book is correct according to the records available to me, it is primarily an impression of the life and work of a man whose influence was of such tremendous significance to me that my first contact with him marked a turning point in my life. Because of this close association, this account of the life of Joel Goldsmith is inevitably filtered through my own experience with him over those eventful years and is replete with personal incidents, all of which show the character of the man and are an integral part of the spiritual journey of Joel Goldsmith. Therefore, I ask the reader's forbearance in what may at times seem to be too frequent reference to myself, because whatever material has been used serves only to illustrate the way in which this man faced life situations and to show how the spiritual principles set forth in the message of The Infinite Way were evolving in his consciousness.

Many friends have played a part in the making of this book. To these I give grateful acknowledgment: Emma A. Goldsmith for permission to quote and use material from the tape recordings and writings of Joel Goldsmith; Bettie Boos Burkhart for her indefatigable work, almost around the clock, typing the work sheets; Margaret Wacker Davis for typing the manuscript in final form; and Gwen Freer Sharer for reading the manuscript and for her invaluable suggestions. To my sister Valborg Sinkler Crossland who has worked faithfully, devotedly, and with great dedication side by side with me in the preparation of this book as she has with all the books of Joel S. Goldsmith I have edited, my gratitude is beyond measure. The importance and value of her assistance can never be fully expressed. For all these persons who have been such beautiful transparencies of Consciousness unfolding and fulfilling Itself, I am most grateful.

L.S.

Juno Beach, Florida

 Prologue

It was the 28th day of September, 1949, for me just another day and another routine appointment. There was little expectation that the day would have any special meaning or that anything would come of that five o'clock meeting. So many such interviews had been fruitless, not only fruitless, but frustrating and disappointing.

Almost seven years before this I had realized that my search for ultimate Reality must be aided and the way pointed out by a teacher who could take me to that final step which I had begun to suspect was the goal of life. That no slightest opportunity to find that one teacher should be passed by, I not only studied the religious announcements in the Saturday newspapers to see who was coming to the city, but I went to hear everyone who purported to have any kind of a spiritual message and, if possible, arranged for an appointment with each one to be sure that I would not judge hastily and thereby miss my great opportunity.

And there were all kinds: sincere, inept, uninspired men and women, some preying upon an undiscerning public, unenlightened but ambitious persons, sometimes somewhat pathetic in their ignorance. Nearly all of them made great promises, but instinctively I felt that their promises were nothing more than that. An inner intuition enabled me very quickly to separate those persons who were sincere, even though they had nothing for me, from those who were charlatans.

So when I drove some thirty miles from Highland Park down to the Loop in Chicago to see Joel Goldsmith, there was little anticipation that this would mark the end of my search for a teacher. Promptly at the appointed hour of five o'clock I opened the door of a small room to find a short, stocky man pacing up and down, wondering why his last appointment had not arrived minutes before the scheduled time, quite typical of a man who wanted tomorrow's work finished yesterday.

A cursory glance at this man would reveal little to the casual observer. Quite unprepossessing to look at, perhaps the one thing about him that stood out most was his piercing eyes that seemed to see right through a person. He had a shock of thick, rather wavy hair, black but with a sprinkling of gray throughout. He was immaculately dressed, and his custom of wearing a string tie, black and tied in a small bow, with long ends hanging down, further distinguished him from most other men.

Nearly fifty people had come to see him that day, and each one had been allotted about ten minutes. But because so many of the appointments were even less than ten minutes, he had finished early, probably weary of those who came, some eagerly, some desperately, with lists of things they wanted to get, while none or few came for what he really had to give. As I walked in, I found myself wondering what I could say to such a man. Most of his sixteen years as a practitioner of spiritual healing must have been spent listening to people who went to him for help with various kinds of problems. But I had no problem, no problem except the big one of wanting to know God. How could I say this to a complete and total stranger? It seemed too sacred to reveal to someone I had never met before and whom I might never see again.

As I sat down, in order to hide my real purpose, I thought of something about which I could ask for spiritual help and quickly stated it. Without saying a word, this quiet man closed his eyes and sat in an attitude of meditation for perhaps five minutes. When he opened his eyes, he looked at me and asked, "What is God?"

That was quite unexpected, and I found myself hesitating and halting, although I had already devoted years and years to the search for God and probably knew most of the words used to describe the Unknowable. To name It was something I could not do. There were no words until finally, shyly and almost apologetically, the words came, "I am a part of God—"

"Oh, no, you are not!" he interrupted me emphatically. "You are the fullness of God." This was all that was necessary, and somehow or other we found ourselves talking animatedly about God and the spiritual path and the Way. For about an hour! As I left, he urged me to keep in touch with him, and this contact which began then has never been broken.

When the interview was terminated, I knew that I had found the teacher for whom I had been searching, and a strange kind of irrepressible joy filled my whole being. It was past six o'clock and, although I felt as if I had wings on my feet and certainly had no need or desire for such a down-to-earth thing as food, nevertheless, my sister, a friend, and I went out for dinner immediately after this appointment. When the waitress came up to serve us—a totally strange and unknown person—she turned to me and said, "Congratulations on your birthday."

"But it's not my birthday," I responded.

"It must be something special because I feel so much joy."

She was right; it was my *real* birthday, the day when I caught a glimpse of my Self and Its potentialities. There was joy then, as there has been from that day on and forever. My feet have walked over some rough places, very rocky ones, but that inner joy has remained, and somehow the vision has continued to soar high above the rocks, the lions, and the tigers of this world.

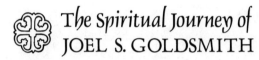

The Spiritual Journey of
JOEL S. GOLDSMITH

I

Beginnings: Human and Spiritual

How does a person tell the story of a man who defies description, but in whose presence one felt stirred to reach for Something beyond the limited horizon of this three-dimensional world? It is a well-nigh impossible task to portray a living soul such as that. Yet this story of a modern mystic whose work has affected deeply the lives of thousands of persons must be told.

His beginnings and early life gave little indication of the fire within him which was to ignite a light in so many whose lives he touched. How could a man who, in his first thirty-six years, had lived a completely worldly life become a mystic and a spiritual teacher, both healing and teaching from the mystical state of consciousness? What a journey! From traveling salesman to mystic! A man with only an eighth grade education, the author of some thirty books!

A publisher in Germany who asked permission to publish his writings in German said that many men wrote books *about* mysticism, but Joel Goldsmith was one of the few men who not only wrote about it, but who was himself a mystic with his entire work stemming from the mystical experience.

Over and over again Joel Goldsmith told me that when

I wrote his biography there was to be a minimum of factual data because that was not the measure of the man: what counted was what he was and his work. Always the work was the most important consideration to him. Joel knew that someday someone would write his life story, and he hoped it would be written by a person who had been close enough to him to understand his work. It was for this reason that he sent me approximately eight pages setting forth what he considered the essential biographical data necessary, along with the following letter:

October 11, 1957

Dear Lorraine:

This is a skeleton. At each major point I will elaborate, but wished you to see what is in thought. All comments welcome.

Love,

Joel

Interestingly enough, the material he sent was written in the third person, and in it of his antecedents he wrote as follows:

Joel Goldsmith was born in New York City on March 10, 1892. His parents were also born in New York City, his father on March 10, 1872, and his mother on October 10, 1872. His mother's parents were both English and came to the United States sometime during or before the Civil War. They were singers in opera, and her father was a cigar maker by trade. He was associated with Samuel Gompers in the organization of the first trade union in the United States in the tobacco industry, but being sensitive by nature, he could not stand the rough and tumble of unionism and soon left that activity.

His father's mother was a German girl who came to the United States when she was nine years of age. His father's father was from Holland. There is no record of when he came to the United States. He passed on when Joel's father was two years of age. Joel's mother lost her mother at nine years of age, so both parents of Joel were brought up in the Hebrew Orphan Asylum in New York City, the mother until about the age of ten and the father until the age of thirteen, when he went out to carve his own way in life. Joel's parents married in New York City in 1891. Joel was their first child; he had a brother two years and four months younger than he and a sister two years younger than the brother.

There was nothing particularly unusual about his birth or early life, nothing to point the direction future years would take. Like all babies, he came into the world crying lustily, but unlike most of them, according to his mother, he continued crying for two years. Later he said it must have been because he took one quick look at the world about him and found it not to his liking.

According to family tradition, he was named Joel Sol Goldsmith because the firstborn son was called either Joel Sol or Sol Joel, depending upon the name of the father. His grandfather was Joel Sol, his father Sol Joel, so he became Joel Sol. It was a name of which he was so proud that even on his elementary school papers he never omitted the middle name Sol, nor as a young adult would he even permit the "S" to be omitted when his name was written. After his first spiritual experience, however, the "S" did not interest him any more and he stopped using it except for legal purposes. Later even his last name dropped away, and the only name he used was Joel. Everyone who knew him called him Joel, and gradually it came about that as he wrote "Joel," the signature seemed to be complete.

His life was probably like that of most youngsters of that age and time, even though, young as he was, he later confessed to feeling a certain sense of detachment and even sadness about the world into which he had been thrust by birth, a feeling not usually found in children.

After Joel's father left the orphanage, he began working for $3.50 a week, but about ten years later while in his twenties, his importing business was yielding him an income of from $12,000 to $15,000 a year, quite a substantial amount for the early 1900's. The family lived on Riverside Drive in a tastefully furnished ten-room apartment with three baths and paid the awesome rental of $125 a month.

Their home life was pleasant, especially when the father was away on business. They gathered as a closely knit family group each night for dinner, followed by a game of bridge. This routine was broken by frequent visits to the theater and the opera.

A housekeeper and a houseman, who doubled as a chauffeur, maintained the apartment, thus freeing Joel's mother for charitable work, which occupied much of her time. Her other great interest lay in music, stemming perhaps from her parents' interest in music and from her years as a protégée of Walter Damrosch, the famous musician and music critic. In 1957 and 1958, when I spent several months in the home of the Goldsmiths in Hawaii, I often found myself humming some bit from one of my favorite operas, which brought forth this response from Joel: "That's like my mother. She, too, went about our home singing all day long."

A very close relationship existed between Joel and his mother, a bond that he felt had begun in some lifetime other than this. In spite of their closeness, however, a credibility gap almost developed between them when one day, shortly before Christmas, his mother told him that there was no Santa Claus and so there was no use for him to hang up his stocking. She took him around to the various department stores to prove it. Every store had a Santa Claus. As they went from store to store she said, "You see, there is no Santa Claus. He is just a man made up to look like Santa Claus."

Of this Joel later said, "My mother didn't convince me at all, so I hung up my stocking just in case." He went on to make the point that no one can convince us that our convictions due to early conditioning are wrong, just as no one can convince us that the God of our ancestors does not exist. We have to outgrow these ingrained concepts ourselves and we have to do it consciously, which is not easy to do.

Since his father traveled extensively in the course of his business, Joel, as the elder son, and his mother spent much time together. Every Friday and Saturday night he would take her out to dinner and to the theater, all dressed up in a little tuxedo suit she had ordered made for him when he was just past thirteen.

Then the day came when he had to travel, and he began to write her a letter every day, seven days a week, a portent of his proclivity for letter writing in later years. Throughout their entire experience together he said that there was hardly a day when he did not write her a letter. They were not always mailed each day, but there were times when she received as many as five letters at once.

When she left his visible sight, it was a moment of complete torture for him. He knew then what it was to lose his God because at that time there was no God closer to him than his mother.

On many occasions during the years I knew him, Joel spoke of his early life, often remarking about how little there was in it outwardly to give any indication of what his life was to become. He wondered how he could have lived two such completely different lives in the same lifetime. In 1958 in Chicago he said:

> How could this happen: What could make such a thing happen? Then I go back inside and I say, "Is that really true? Am I not now the person that I always was, but couldn't show outwardly because I didn't know how to reach it? Isn't this what I always longed for? Isn't this what I always visioned but couldn't break through?"
>
> I know the answer. I can go all the way back and hear my mother saying, "I know what's wrong with you, Joel. You are looking for God."
>
> I said, "Mom, how can you say that? I don't even know if there is a God."
>
> "Oh, but I know that you are looking for God."
>
> Certainly I was, and this life today is just the fruition. I came into this world looking for God. You can't tell it if you look at my first thirty-eight years. It was all locked up inside of me. I wouldn't have dared tell that to anybody except my own mother. Later, when I was nineteen, I did tell my mother, "I have discovered you are right. There is a God, but I can't find Him. No matter to whom I talk, they don't seem to know Him."
>
> And she said, "Well, please don't stop, and when you find Him, come and tell me." And I hope I am telling her.[1]

It was a very tender moment in that Chicago class when Joel told this incident long after his mother had gone on.

While Joel's mother and father were God-fearing people of Hebrew ancestry, they were not practicing Jews, and Joel was never taught any of the precepts of the Judaic faith except that all the children were given instruction in the Ten Commandents. Holy days, such as the Day of Atonement and Passover, were observed in what would be considered a very unsatisfactory manner by orthodox Jews; that is, the Goldsmith family observed these days by recognizing that the Jews were observing them. They did not go to temple or synagogue, and if they had matzoth in the home at Passover, it was only because they enjoyed eating them.

For this family the two principal holidays in the year were Christmas and Easter, not for any religious reason, but because they all liked to give and receive gifts, and these holidays gave them a good excuse for gift-giving. So for the first few years of Joel's life there was no formal religious training whatever with the exception of "the advice from my mother that obeying the Ten Commandments would keep me out of trouble, make me a decent citizen, and if I had an interest then in religious subjects, I could follow out my search in any way that opened to me, without being handicapped by any one religious teaching."[2]

When Joel was a little past twelve, his mother told him that someday he might want to know more about the different churches and religions in the world and especially about God. If he wanted to begin, he could have the opportunity to gain some of that knowledge in the Jewish temple because, traditionally, at thirteen a boy in the Jewish faith takes on the responsibilites of manhood, and then is supposed to begin deciding his future. At about twelve and a half years, therefore, he was sent to a Reform Jewish temple and given some instruction so that he could be confirmed at thirteen. To him confirmation was an unpleasant experience; he rebelled against the kind of prayers uttered on that day, and he never went back to temple afterwards except many years later when a customer, while he was on the road, insisted on taking him there one holiday.

In 1907 he met a young German boy who was in New York for

the purpose of learning English, and who later returned home for business reasons. Out of this meeting grew a friendship which lasted for forty-nine years, a bond so strong that in later years Joel recognized it as a spiritual relationship.

In all those years there was never a misunderstanding between them, years in which there were occasions when if Joel needed money it was always available from Hans, while Hans would always find Joel ready to share with him. During those forty-nine years of friendship in which two wars divided them and in which Hans was on the German side and Joel on the American side, never for one minute was the bond between them broken. When Hans passed on, he paid Joel the honor of leaving his family, a widow with three children, to his care. They continued to be his family and Joel a part of their family. He saw that they did not lack, and every year that he went to Germany he visited them.

Joel completed the eighth grade, but his formal schooling terminated after a few months in high school, due to an argument he had with the principal. Even those first eight years were frequently interrupted when he played hooky to steal away to matinee performances of Shakespeare at a nearby theater. Then as always the theater had a tremendous fascination for him. Years later, in fact, when he was conducting an Infinite Way class in Los Angeles, he found himself quoting Shakespeare accurately on the subject of defamation of character, adding proudly, "Not bad after fifty-four years!"

The very day Joel quit school, his father began to teach him all that he knew about the importing business. A few years after that, when he was sixteen and a half, Joel was taken to Europe on a buying expedition as an assistant to his father, who was a buyer of European laces and allied lines of merchandise. To this work Joel brought an innate intuitive faculty that knew exactly the right laces to buy at the right time. So his travels began, at first in connection with the business world that was to occupy him for the early part of his life.

Joel's father had begun to travel to Europe on business about 1900. Whenever the father made a trip, a little black case had to be taken down to the drug store to be filled with bicarbonate of soda, other aids to digestion, and aspirin. There were twelve remedies that had to be ready for each trip, and the little black case usually came home practically empty. In fact there was so much illness in the family when he was a child that at one time Joel wanted to become a doctor and began reading medical books.

In 1915 on one of these buying trips his father became ill, was taken off a ship at Southampton, and rushed to Nottingham, where he was in a hospital seventy-seven days. Then the cable came, "Goldsmith dying. Send for body." This news, of course, created pandemonium in the household, and in the confusion that followed Joel took charge, arranged the details, and saw his mother off to England.

That night Joel had an engagement to take a friend to dinner, so he decided that he should call at her home and explain the situation. When he arrived there, he met her father, to whom he confided that he had put his mother on a steamer that afternoon to go to Europe to bring back his father's body. The conversation as Joel described it ran somewhat like this:

The girl's father then asked, "When did your father die?"

"He is not dead yet but he is dying or he may be dead by now," and Joel showed him the cable.

"Oh, no," he said, "you are a very young man, and your father must be comparatively young, too. He doesn't have to die."

To Joel that seemed a strange comment. "He doesn't have to die? The doctors say so. He has been in the hospital for seventy-seven days."

"Well, have you ever heard of prayer and prayer healing?"

"No, the only prayer I know is 'Now I lay me down to sleep.' Do you mean Christian Science?"

"Yes."

"Mind over matter! I've read about that in the paper. You don't really think that that would help anybody, do you?"

"I am a Christian Science practitioner, and I do believe it."

This came as almost as much of a shock to Joel as the cable had been. But his courteous reply was, "If you can help him, of course, do so. It would be a marvelous thing if he could come home."

The practitioner did not try to explain the principle involved to

Joel or probably he would not even have asked him to help his father. He thought the practitioner was just going to pray to God, and if he were holy enough maybe God would answer him. Joel knew nothing about healing by prayer but felt that it could do no harm. Certainly it did no harm because when Joel's mother landed in England his father was up, dressed, and ready to go home, and for twenty-five years after that knew very little of illness, even surviving his wife by a number of years.

The miraculous recovery of his father led Joel to begin a desultory study of Christian Science, in which he sought answers to the questions that naturally arose in the mind of a person who had traveled the world as he had, questions that kept plaguing him with an urgency that drove him on.

On his first trip to Europe in 1909, when the German and the English fleets were facing each other in the North Sea and he heard the newsboys on the streets of London calling out their "Extra! Extra!" telling of the imminence of war, he began to wonder where God was in all that. Then a few weeks later his father took him to Paris and wisely showed him the darkest and most wicked side of night life in Paris which the father thought could serve only to disgust Joel so that he would have no illusions about it and not believe that it was something attractive or glamorous. Again his thought went to the question: Where is God? How do men and women get into this condition, with all the churches in the world and all the praying?

My entire family background is Hebrew, and never in my life had I known anything of a Christian teaching. In fact, I had never known anything of any teaching except the Ten Commandments. But when I was nineteen, whether it was the Voice or an impression, Something within me said, "Find the man Jesus, and you will have the secret of life." That was a strange thing to say to me because I knew nothing of Jesus Christ beyond the name and that Christmas was a holiday celebrating his birth. But from that minute on my life has been dedicated to that man Jesus and his secret.

Six months after that, this Voice or impression said, "Become a Mason and learn about God." I knew nothing about Masonry, and there was no one in my family who knew anything about it. So I learned that I would be eligible to join a Masonic Order when I was twenty-one. My business associate helped me become a Mason, and the Voice fulfilled Itself in Its promise because the first night in the Masonic Lodge, I learned something about God that I had never known before and also something about prayer.[3] I was given the First Degree the week after I was twenty-one, and at twenty-two I had my Thirty-second Degree.

At that First Degree of initiation, I was presented with a Bible, and while I had been traveling since I was sixteen and a half years of age and had seen many Gideon Bibles in hotel rooms, believe it or not, this was the first time I ever knew what a Bible was. So you see I was pretty ignorant of religion, and of course I had never studied anything in the way of philosophy or anything of that kind because my school days ended with six months of high school. . . . So I had no knowledge of philosophy or religion, and yet all the time I was searching, searching for something we call God. It was from then on that this search for God or this search for an answer to the mystery of life became active within me.[4]

All his life Joel maintained a serious interest in Masonry and kept a close association with the Masonic Order. In 1923 he received an honorary membership in a Masonic Lodge in Germany, and of his work in Masonry, Darcy Lodge of New York City wrote the following on the program introducing him when he gave a talk there on May 12, 1958:

Brother Joel S. Goldsmith was raised in Darcy Lodge on February 13, 1914. . . . During World War I, Brother Goldsmith was a founder and president of the Marines' Masonic Club of Quantico, Virginia. His services as such received the recognition of several 33rd Degree and KCCH Masons in Washington.

In later years he became vitally interested in Esoteric Masonry and the work of Wilmhurst, giving talks on this little understood subject to many different lodges. In 1957 he was made an honorary member of the Lodge of Living Stones #4957, of Leeds, England. His Scottish Rite affiliation was in Honolulu where he was a member of the Aloha Temple Shrine, and where on several different occasions he gave the Maundy Thursday and Easter Sunday work for the Scottish Rite Body.

When the United States entered World War I, Joel, in his enthusiasm to "lick the Kaiser," volunteered in the Marines. He was stationed at Parris Island and there underwent the rigorous training to which Marines are subjected.

During this time he served as Second Reader in a Christian Science Society organized for a little group of Marines. There were many long hours of pondering on how it was possible to follow the teaching of the Master, Christ Jesus, and go out and kill. It was then that the Bible, which was at his bedside, dropped on the floor and opened to the passage, "Neither pray I for these alone."

In that moment the passage was illumined for him, and he saw the mistaken zeal in the practice of the churches that opened their doors to pray for victory while none of them was praying for the enemy. Suddenly he knew that the only righteous or effectual prayer anyone could pray is the prayer for the enemy, a form of prayer which from that moment on he began to practice diligently.

Shortly thereafter his platoon was divided in half on the basis of a numbering-off system. One-half of the men were sent to Europe where nearly all of them perished in the Battle of Château-Thierry. The other half remained to be given further artillery practice. Joel, along with a young corporal named Perry Wheeler who knew him well in those days and who many years later became the husband of my sister Swanhild, remained in the United States and never had to fire a shot at anyone.

Sitting in the Wheeler living room one day early in July of 1958 and looking at some snapshots my sister Valborg was going to incorporate in a family album for Swanhild and Perry, our eyes lighted upon a picture of our brother-in-law and three other Marines. Valborg and I looked questioningly at each other as our eyes fell upon the third man in the picture and as Perry retold that same story of the division of the men in his platoon into two groups.

When we asked Perry who this man was, he casually told us that his name was Goldsmith, but did not recall his given name. Furthermore, on the Masonic program Perry had saved from his Parris Island days a bugler by the name of Julius Goldsmith was listed, but no Joel Goldsmith. It did not add up although the likeness of the man in the picture to Joel was so great and the stories so identical that we had a duplicate made, which I hesitatingly sent to Joel in London with the query as to who these men were and if he might possibly be one of them. His reply was like the man and showed his delightful sense of humor better than any descriptive words could possibly do:

July 25, 1958

Dear Lorraine:

You shock me! Even if you did not know the name, how you could possibly not recognize me—since I have hardly changed even a tiny bit since then? I just looked in the mirror and I truly believe this is a photo of me taken very, very recently, with the others dubbed in! Of course, that is Joel, buck private in the rear ranks—10 Regt—Artillery Quantico, Va.—Associate Editor of the Quantico Leatherneck, Second Reader of C. S. Services, and President and Chairman of the Board, Marines Masonic Club, Quantico. On one side is Corp. Wheeler, on the other is Estes, and on his side is the brains whose name this instant eludes me, but it will come back as I knew him well.

Now where did you unearth this? Is Wheeler still about? Or Estes? The latter had a brother with us.

I understand your query—how could one as young as Joel have been in that photo in 1918? How my past rises up! . . .

Love,

Joel

After the war was over Joel found that it marked the end of an era for the world as well as for his father's importing business. By this time handmade dresses had become almost obsolete and mass production of clothing had taken over. Handmade imported lace was no longer in demand, and Joel was called upon to try to hold together the family business. In this effort he failed, and the business collapsed.

In addition to business difficulties he became critically ill with tuberculosis and was given three months to live. Since there was no medical hope, he decided that he would seek help from a Christian Science practitioner, which he did, and in three months he made a complete recovery. When Joel was telling of this experience a few years ago, a skeptic insisted that a wrong diagnosis had been made and that Joel had never had such a thing, because if he had, it could not have been cured. Joel agreed to submit to an X-ray examination, which showed that he had only one lung, but where the other lung should have been, there was, as he described it to me, a wall of muscle.

After the family business collapsed, Joel once more became a traveling man, selling different kinds of articles, most of them in some way connected with women's apparel. Even then, before he had been touched by any kind of spiritual experience, his attitude toward selling was quite different from that of the average salesman, which is perhaps why he was so successful.

The firm that he represented sent him to Pittsburgh to take over that territory for a year. His first call was upon a buyer in the largest department store in the area, and the first thing she said after he introduced himself was, "No, I don't need anything."

"Well, of course, you don't know me, so would you mind if I explained a little about myself?" He went on to tell her that he would be there for a year in accordance with his contract. That meant that he would be calling on her twice a month for about nine months out of the year, eighteen times in all. "Each time I'm going to come in and call on you. If you say to me, 'No, I don't need anything,' I'll either walk out or talk to you about something else.

But never will I say, 'Will you reconsider?' or 'I have something else.' "

She looked at him and said, "You will never make good as a salesman. You know a salesman's work only begins when the buyer says, 'No.' "

"You've met an entirely different type of salesman. I know what I have in my trunk. I have a marvelous line of merchandise. It is as important for the buyer to have it as it is for me to sell it, and it is up to the buyer to know that. So I will offer it with all the love in my heart, and if the buyer doesn't want it, that will be all right with me, too."

In his entire territory that year, that buyer became Joel's best customer because she came to realize he was telling her the truth. He had unbounded confidence in what he had to sell; he knew that it was good; and he knew it was good for her. It might not be good for her department every time he called, but it was a good article, and on that basis he worked.

Even in those early days Joel was intuitively aware of certain spiritual principles, and so he recognized that when a salesman goes into a business house to sell, normally the buyer immediately puts up a defense, and then the salesman is supposed to break down that defense. If a salesman, however, were to go into a business house in the realization that he had a good product and that if the buyer needed it today, it was available to him, and if he didn't need it that was all right too, the buyer would feel that the salesman was not coming there to make a sale, but coming to be of service.

Of this period of his life, while he was selling on the road, endlessly traveling, Joel sent me a notation which he had written in Hawaii on July 11, 1963:

> My life has been told in two Bible passages: "My kingdom is not of this world" and "I have meat to eat that ye know not of." At no time have I known pleasure, or profit, or success in "this world." There was no interest in school except in the reading of books.

In my years of business and travel, there were no delights. Business was merely a livelihood, and travel was a means to that end.

And in family life, which was surely above the average in comfort and fellowship, there was no pleasure, no joy, no satisfaction. I still have no awareness of what kept me going on the fruitless rounds of days and nights because there was no hope of attaining anything better.

There were many years of trying to lose myself in theaters, restaurants, and night clubs in New York, Paris, Berlin, and many other cities, but these pleasures were but means of forgetting.

Strange, indeed, and unhappy is the life devoid of human satisfaction and means of human peace, more especially when no thought of possible spiritual joys and victories enters in. Even when I sought for spiritual knowledge there was no hope or sense that fulfillment would come. In fact, how could I know the meaning of fulfillment?

This chapter is no gloomier to hear than my life was to live, although this could not have been visible to those around me. Always there was a sufficiency of the things money will buy, always lots of baubles and bangles.

What must have appeared outwardly as a very mediocre life was passed with no deep drama and certainly no light comedy until That Day when, in meditation with an acquaintance, the veil was lifted, and I entered another world, actually another state of consciousness.

It seemed like a dream world, because I went through the motions of daily living without any apparent change. Yet the whole outer experience was as if walking through a dream. Many who came to me seeking healing, for no known reason, received it although I know not how or why.

Although Joel was a master salesman and very successful for a number of years, a time came when his business became less and less, diminishing to the point of no return, even with all the spiritual help that he sought. Still at this time he had no thought of anything other than a business career. It was during that period that he contracted a very bad cold. What happened he tells in his own words:

> I was taken sick in the city of Detroit, went to a building that was filled with Christian Science practitioners, found the name of a practitioner on the board, went up to this man's office, and asked him to help me. He told me that it was Saturday and that he didn't take patients on Saturday. That day he always spent in meditation and prayer.
>
> To this I said, "Of course you wouldn't turn me out looking the way I do," and I really was looking bad.
>
> "No, come on in."
>
> And I went in, and he permitted me to stay there two hours with him. He talked to me of the Bible; he talked to me of truth. Long before the two hours were up, I was healed of that cold, and when I went out on the street I found I couldn't smoke any more. When eating my dinner I found I couldn't drink any more. The following week I found I couldn't play cards any more, and I also found that I couldn't go to the horse races any more. And the businessman had died.[5]
>
> Within thirty-six hours after my first spiritual experience, a woman buyer who was a customer of mine said that if I would pray for her she would be healed. The only prayer I knew at that moment was "Now I lay me down to sleep," and I didn't see that that was going to do much healing.
>
> But she insisted that if I would pray for her she would be healed and there was nothing for me to do but pray. So I closed my eyes, and I am happy to say that I have always been honest with God. I said, "Father, You know that I don't know how to pray, and I certainly know nothing about healing. So if there is anything I should do, tell me."
>
> And very, very clearly, as much so as if I were hearing a voice, I realized that man is not a healer. That satisfied me.

That was the extent of my praying, but the woman had her healing, a healing of alcoholism.

The next day a traveling salesman came in and said, "Joel, I don't know what your religion is, but I do know that if you pray for me, I could get well."

What are you going to do about that? Argue? No. "Let's close our eyes and pray." And so I closed my eyes and said, "Father, here's another customer!" But while my eyes were closed and nothing was happening, the salesman touched me and said, "Wonderful, the pain is gone."[6]

That was a daily experience. The only problem was that I had too few customers and too many patients. A transformation had taken place. Where had it taken place? It had taken place in my consciousness, not anywhere else, not outside. It was the same individual whose whole thought had been on business and pleasure. All of a sudden his whole thought was on God and healing, the same individual, only with a transformation such as took place in the experience of Moses, a realization of true identity, an experience that must have taken place in the minds of many others before and since.[7]

From this moment on there were two men. There was Joel, an individual always hovering around somewhere in the background, but showing tendencies which continuously led to many human mistakes, many human errors of judgment, many human discords, but fortunately only apparent to himself at intervals. On the other hand, there was the individual who on that day of revelation or regeneration was ordained within as a spiritual healer.[8]

From that day to this I have paid respect to the practitioner for having been responsible for the entire change in my life and for all that has happened to me in a spiritual way since then. . . . It is true that my thirteen years of work prepared me for such an experience, but his was the touch that brought about the transformation. It was he who changed my life, he who was accustomed to spend one whole day every week without taking a patient, without attempting to earn a dollar, without attempting to use spiritual power, one whole day a week in every week just to renew and fulfill himself with the Spirit. And look what that practice of spending a day like that did for me![9]

2

🧠 The Preparation

And so the businessman in Joel died. Although five Christian Science practitioners had been helping him at various times so that his business would improve, it continued to dwindle until finally he found himself penniless. Strangely enough, though, with this failure of his business, many business acquaintances began asking him to pray for them, which was certainly a twist. By this time Joel had entered upon a serious study of Christian Science: he joined the church and took class instruction.

One morning after Joel's partner told him that he had had twenty-two calls and not one from a customer, he took the partner's advice, went uptown, and opened an office to engage in the healing ministry under the banner of Christian Science. His resources were so depleted that he did not have an extra dime to his name and, in order to embark on this new venture, he had to borrow $250, using $125 for rent and the other $125 for living expenses. His hope had been that through prayer he would be able to see God's hand manifest in more orders, but as he said years later, God paid no attention to him or to the five very good practitioners who had been helping him. Joel did not understand how God could have done this to him, but he recognized that the will of God does not operate according to the stupidity or personal will of man.

Shortly after he had become a member of a Christian Science branch church in New York, a young man came to him and said that he was serving as usher at the Christian Science Services in Rikers Island Prison and wanted to go on vacation but would not be able to go unless a substitute could be provided. He explained to Joel what the work entailed, and asked him if he would like to substitute for him, to which Joel replied that he would be interested.

The young man went to the chairman of the committee who had charge of the prison work, and when the chairman was told the name of the proposed substitute, she said, "Oh, no, he is not your substitute; he is my reader."

"What do you mean?"

"That is my demonstration. We have an opening for a reader at the prison service. I knew the reader would be supplied, and the other night the name Goldsmith came to me. I didn't know any Goldsmith and didn't know what connection it had with our reader. But the man you have met is my Goldsmith, and he is our reader."

Usually before such an appointment could be made one had to have an audition to prove that he would be satisfactory, but Joel immediatley received a three-year appointment over the telephone simply because the chairman had had a dream of a man named Goldsmith as the reader.

Joel was told to spend a great deal of time doing "protective work" against sin-filled thoughts before each service he read. So he worked diligently from Friday night to Sunday morning, but the more work of this type he did, the more difficult his job became until he realized that Christ was the mind of these men and that Christ was the only identity with which he was faced.

After that the attendance grew rapidly at the prison service, and the work progressed so well that soon some of the prisoners were doing healing work inside the prison. All this took place within a period of two years, Joel said, by a conscious act of forgiving, not saying, "Oh, you sinner, I will let you off." That is not forgiving. The forgiving was real forgiveness: "Thy sins be forgiven thee." Now let us start all over and let me recognize your true identity and no longer feel that I am more righteous than you, but rather that spiritually we are one."

The men in the prison who had enough spiritual attunement were drawn to that service. Interestingly enough, on Thanksgiving morning one could hear the guards going through the prison, announcing services of the various church denominations and that free gifts such as cigarettes and candy would be distributed. Following this came the announcement, "Eleven o'clock, Christian Science Service. No free gifts." But there was still a full attendance without free gifts because there was this act of forgiveness, this act of understanding.

Forgiveness as a principle of life, the first glimpse of which came to him as a Marine, played an important part in Joel's practice and life. Its efficacy was demonstrated in the case of a man who was an architect and builder, with his work largely in the area of building Christian Science churches and luxury homes for those in the upper income bracket. During the depression of 1929 he lost everything he had, and he and his wife, in order to support themselves, went out to do Christian Science nursing.

One day he turned to Joel, asking for spiritual help in order to collect a large sum of money someone owed him. If he could collect that money, he felt it would be enough to carry him through the depression. Could Joel help him collect it?

God very quickly gave Joel the words, "No, I can't, and if I could I wouldn't, because maybe the man who owes you the money is in a worse position than you are and, in taking it from him, you might be depriving him or his wife or children or grandchildren. I am not interested in helping you collect your money but I can give you spiritual help."

"How?"

"Well, I don't know. Let's see." And as they sat for a few moments in meditation, the answer came to Joel out of the Lord's Prayer, " 'Forgive us our debts as we forgive our debtors.' There's your answer. Forgive this man his debt, and you will be forgiven your lack."

"That's the only thing I've got left."

"No," Joel said, "you are in the position of a lot of us. God is the only thing you have left. Everything else has flown, so let's see what God can do. Actually God can't do anything: God is doing all He can do, but you and I can do something, and that is to come into harmony with the law. We have been given the law in accord with the Lord's Prayer, the prayer of law. And what is the law? Forgive me as I forgive others."

The man, desperate as he was, agreed to try to put this principle into practice and to forgive his debtor. "I am not going to say anything to him. If he wants to pay it, he can; but as far as I am concerned, that is dead. Now if I am to live, I will have to live through the grace of God. I will have no more reliance on anything in this human world."

That night he was called upon to help design a building, and his check for his work on that project was not only enough for him to live on for two weeks but also to pay up a few back debts. When the two weeks were up he received a call from Long Island and was asked, "Are you the architect who designed a Christian Science Church in 1919 that has never been built?"

"Yes, I am that man."

"Well, now we are ready to build it." He started the building, and at the same time he was called to New Jersey to begin work on a government project. In two years he was a partner in a building and construction company. True, this man was a capable person, but the point is that the miracle took place not through anything that was in a book, not through reading the Lord's Prayer, but through acting upon it, through an act of consciousness.

The sick—those sick, physically, mentally, morally, and financially —came to Joel and found release. He was driven by a tremendous force within him that would not let him rest. Hour after hour he studied, prayed, and studied.

> At the beginning of my work, I did not know truth. . . .
> When I began healing work, it was by closing my eyes, just
> sitting there quietly waiting. A deep breath would come to me,
> and the patient was very quickly healed. In those days most of

the healings were quick ones and many of them instantaneous, but there was no knowledge behind my work. There was only the gift of the Spirit.[1]

In his early days of study Joel would spend four, five, and six hours a day with concordances, the Bible, and Mary Baker Eddy's writings, poring over them and then meditating. He soon found out which Christian Science lecturers had the Spirit and would go to hear them, often attending three or four lectures a week. It was not always that he felt that what they said was absolute truth, but there was enough realized consciousness in these lecturers to help break down the resistance to truth that is in most of us by birth.

Those early days of the practice were difficult ones. Far from improving his condition, Joel found his situation considerably worsened:

If I had been looking for supply, I will tell you truthfully, I found more lack than I had ever known before. If I had been looking for health, I didn't find it; and if I had been looking for home and companionship, I can tell you that I was down to no friends and no home.

When the spiritual light touched me, it took from me everything in my human world: position, income, friends, family, home, and money. It was a housecleaning, and I am sure that some of my former friends looked at my experience and, knowing that I was trying to make a spiritual demonstration, must have said that they would rather get along without God. I can hardly blame them, judging from appearances, because the outer picture was bleak, and it wasn't bleak for only a week or two.

As far as I was concerned, I wasn't aware of the outer picture except that it was happening, but it wasn't touching me because inside something wonderful had taken place. I had really left this world and come into a realization of "*My** kingdom," and so I probably wasn't as aware as my friends were of all the lacks

*My and Me, capitalized, refer to God.

and limitations that I was going through. But the point is that
it was a spiritual experience, a religious experience. It really
was an act of Grace, but it had the effect of what the Master
called overcoming the world, although I don't know if it was
overcoming it or just destroying it because it was bombed out.

For several years it was a hard struggle, years of knowing
friendlessness and what it was to be without family. Yet during
those years healing works were coming through. Other people
were being benefited and blessed, and I am sure that if it hadn't
been that this time just coincided with the beginning of the
Great Depression, those who had benefited would have been
happy to share with me and to express gratitude, but financially
they themselves were going through terrible days and so sharing wasn't easy.

Then, of course, gradually as more and more light came, as
greater awareness came, the situation eased, and finally came
into harmony. But the main point that I am making is this, that
it is difficult to look at the life of those who have been spiritually touched and realize that the land of milk and honey sometimes comes forty years later.[2]

On August 24, 1956, Joel wrote the following in a letter to me
which perhaps sums up his struggles and his attitude toward those
struggles more clearly than anything anyone could say:

Problems—my own problems—have never disturbed me. In
periods of actual lack—there were days when [the corner re-
staurant's] ten cents for coffee and doughnuts was a blessing
and a full day's intake! There was one night of sleeping in the
New York Subway and another in a parked car in January in
New York! But there was no "down-heartedness"— no dis-
couragement—no doubt and no fear. I was the beholder
watching the play go through Acts 1, 2, 3, and 4. There were
always four acts in the ten cent, twenty cent, and thirty cent
melodramas!

And I went through a very serious illness—with no sense of
failure—just the ever-watching to see the next scene of the

present act! Having known both health and abundant supply most of my life—I was not fooled into seeking these. What I wanted far transcended these—and I soon realized the price is high.

Early in this new career of spiritual healing Joel was called to give help to a young Finnish serving girl stricken with tuberculosis. The disease had worked such havoc that the patient had been placed in the death shack of the sanitarium to await death. It took thirteen weeks of consistent prayer work, sometimes ten and twenty times a day, before she was removed from the death shack to the other part of the sanitarium and then another thirteen months before she was released and pronounced cured.

Joel wrote countless letters to her which he maintained she did not understand because of her meager knowledge of English. But she was aware of far more than he realized. In the past few years I have had some correspondence with her, and she has even shared with me parts of his letters to her which she has treasured all these years. Here is one of them which was written in 1933 in New York and which she gave to me just recently:

Dear Friend:

Mrs. Eddy says in S & H,* "In Science, all *being* is *eternal, spiritual, perfect, harmonious, in every action.*" Please look up in your dictionary the meaning of all the words I have underlined, and then remember that you are that being. Also memorize the above statement, which is on page 407:22-24.

Your being is perfect; therefore it includes every quality of perfection which also includes love, friendship, companionship, peace, and freedom. There is no worry, no fear, no fretting, no lack of faith and truth in your being. Your being is the expression of substance, of love, of home.

Thank you for your prayers for me and for my home. God hears every prayer for good, and He answers all prayers. We must remember not to pray for material things, but for spiritual

---

* *Science and Health.*

qualities. Never pray or ask for a well body, a material home or friends, but pray for the understanding of perfection, for spiritual understanding of heaven as home, for harmony, peace, joy, the abundance of all good. Those are the things we pray for, and we receive the outward manifestation in the form of human friends, home, health, etc. Do you understand that?

All good wishes, sincerely,

Joel Goldsmith

The letters Joel wrote, he felt, were not really for the development of her spiritual consciousness but for his own. In them he clarified for himself every principle that could possibly relate to the problem. This particular case proved to be of great significance because it showed him the value of unswerving dedication to a principle. Furthermore, although many cases of tuberculosis were brought to him in the ensuing years, he lost only two of them. The rest were quickly healed.

By this time most of Joel's friends and relatives had all concluded that he was cracked on the subject of truth, and so they would have nothing to do with him because they said he was not sensible. They saw, too, that he who had always been so free and easy with his money now had no money at all to spend.

I conformed to the pattern that most Christian Science practitioners observed. I kept an account book, and in that book the names of everyone who came to my office were entered and everyone who telephoned or wrote to me for help. At the end of the month they were sent statements. Three dollars was charged for each visit to my office and two dollars for each absent treatment whether patients phoned or wrote for it. It was expected that sometime after they received the bill, the patients would pay it.

The first seven months of my practice I was earning enough to support myself, but in this seventh month a strange thing happened. On the tenth of the month I did not have enough money come in to pay all the previous month's bills, and so I looked at my accounts and found that my patients owed me

$150 but I only owed $100 so I was solvent. Everything was all right, and I went to bed and slept peacefully until three o'clock in the morning. Then something woke me up and said, "Hey! hey! What is this? You are perfectly content to sleep because you are owed $150, but you only owe $100?"

"Yes, sure, sure, everything is all right."

"Oh, everything is all right because you are owed $50 more than you owe? God doesn't enter into this picture at all, does He? You don't need God this month, do you?"

"No, I really don't, do I? I have Mrs. Jones, Mrs. Brown, and Mrs. Smith to the tune of $50 to the good."

"Oh, no," It said, "that won't do, Joel. That's not right. That isn't the kind of teaching that you have accepted that you are all right because these people owe you $150. The teaching you have accepted is that you are all right because you have found God."

"That's right."

"Well, haven't you found God without that $150?"

"Certainly."

"It doesn't seem so."

"I need that $150."

So I realized that I might as well make up my mind then and there that I had either found God or I hadn't. If I had found God, I certainly was not dependent upon these things. If I had not found God I had better get out of the practice because I would only be cheating those who came to me.

So I got out of bed, wrote out receipted bills for the $150 and put this note at the bottom of each one, "A beautiful thing has just come into my life for which I wish to express gratitude, so please accept this receipted bill with no questions asked."

I went out in the hall, dropped them into the mailbox, and said, "Now, Father, I still owe $100, but I have nothing but God. And if God isn't adequate, here goes one practitioner out of business."

The next night I went to a church Board Meeting and afterward we went [out] for some coffee or chocolate, so it was after eleven o'clock when I got back to my hotel. There in the lobby, standing against the desk, was a traveling salesman I hadn't seen in thirteen years. He drank a little too heavily in those earlier days, and the last time I saw him he was a little under the weather. I had taken him to my room, sent his clothes out to be pressed, let him sleep all night, and given him some money to get back into his territory in the morning. Then came World War I, and he enlisted and I enlisted and never again did we meet during all those years. But here he was smoking a cigar in the lobby of the hotel, late at night.

"What are you doing here?"

"Well, I'm on my honeymoon, and we came to this small uptown hotel to be away from the big noise downtown. My wife doesn't like smoking, so I have come down to the lobby to smoke before I retire."

We stood talking, and finally he said, "You know, I owe you some money."

"You did," I said, "but it's probably outlawed by now."

His reply was, "What do you mean outlawed? I have nothing to do with the law. I owe you the money. I have never sent it to you as I didn't have your address, and then when it did enter my mind, I thought that there's one man of all men who will never need money." Of course remembering me from the days when he got the money, he might well be able to believe that. So he went on and said, "How much is it, and I will give you a check."

We got our heads together and started a little mathematical thinking, and when we got through we decided that the nearest thing we could tally it with was about $150. Since that time I have never sent out a bill or statement, nor have I ever asked anyone for money.[3]

Supply began to come in gradually, but there was always a sufficiency.

In the early 1930's, after Joel had had considerable success in his work and a goodly measure of prosperity, he married Rose Robb, a brilliant woman with great intellectual capacity, who at one time had been the music critic for a Philadelphia newspaper. She spoke seven languages fluently, but best of all she had a very extensive library which was Joel's first introduction to some of the great masterpieces of literature. He quickly fastened upon Eliot's *Five Foot Bookshelf* and Elbert Hubbard's *Little Journeys* to the homes of famous men, and became acquainted with the books of religionists and philosophers that he had not known existed. He read voraciously into the long hours of the night, maintaining himself on only three and a half hours of sleep.

Since Rose had two children and one of them wanted to attend Harvard, it seemed wise for them to move to Boston, which they did about 1933. Joel's Christian Science teacher, who lived in Boston, discouraged him about making this move, saying, "I can't have you in Boston; you are too good a man. I have plans for you, and you will just break your heart here. You can't make good here."

"What's wrong?"

"Well, this is New England. You have a Jewish name and a Jewish face, and they are not going to like it. New Englanders are very conservative. Furthermore, they don't pay a practitioner enough to support your family the way you want to live."

He went on to tell Joel what some of the practitioners earned in Boston, some of the very good ones. So Joel said, "Well, you have forced me to move to Boston, because to me this is a principle. If it doesn't work in Boston, it isn't a principle. It's got to work even if I were cast out on the ocean or in the desert. If it doesn't, I will have to give this up and go back to business, because business does operate on principle. If you know your product and if you give good service, you can't fail, and I can always go back to business."

"Oh, that would be very foolish."

"All right," was Joel's response. "Let's make it more foolish. For one year I will not go inside of a church or to a lecture or to any place where Christian Scientists gather. I will not permit a Christian Scientist to come into my home unless he is a patient. Furthermore, I will not enter the home of a Christian Scientist unless it is that of a patient to whom I am called. I will go to my office, and I will stay there from nine in the morning until four or five o'clock in the afternoon even if no one comes to me. Then I'll go home. I will stay at home until the next morning in time to get to the office so that no one is going to know that Joel Goldsmith is in Boston and no one is going to know that he is a practitioner. If at the end of the year I do not have a good practice, I am not only going out of the practice, I am going out of Christian Science, too."

Joel's attitude was that if there is God, then he had no problem; if there is no God, he was in for some real trouble. So he sat in his office alone day after day. And what an office it was! A bare room without curtains or carpet. Four gas pipes with a board on top served as a table. There was one kitchen chair and on the radiator a bread-board for the second chair. Four months passed before there was any additional furniture and two years before there was a carpet or a curtain. It was almost as barren as the Manger, this beginning of a worldwide ministry. Yet, as as he sat there alone, he was not alone. This Presence that had been with him since August, 1928, was with him there and became an ever-expanding awareness.

To all intents and appearances it seemed as if he had made a mistake. His healing work continued to be successful, but in spite of that he found himself faced with the problem of maintaining a family with insufficient income all the while he was doing this beautiful healing work, being busy with it day and night, and still not having sufficient return to meet the financial demands made upon him.

One day as he was walking to his office, a distance of three and one-half miles, which he walked back and forth for lack of five cents' carfare, he found himself puzzled as to why this should be. It was then that it came to him very strongly that the only reason he had such a problem was because he did not know God. That was quite a jolt to him after he had been devoting years of his life to the pursuit of God and to helping other people through this God which he now felt he did not know.

It was then that he looked down at his feet and began to realize that he was not in those feet. From there he went to other parts of the body and saw that he, the identity that he was, could not possibly be found any place in the body, nor could he be confined in a body. He saw that he was not a body but that he was Consciousness. He was *I*,* limitless and fetterless *I*, and that *I* was God.

It was revealed to me in my inner work that the *I* is God: *I* is Self-maintaining and Self-sustaining; *I* is the source of supply. So I thought, "Oh, *I AM THAT I AM* means that I embody supply, I include it. It is embraced within my own being. It does not come to me: it flows out from me."

But it was not an hour later before someone asked me to pay a bill that I owed, and I had to give lip service to the appearance by saying, "Certainly, as soon as possible. I haven't it at this moment but the moment it arrives, you will have it," and then to myself saying, "You are a liar because you know that *I* is God and you know that that *I* has sufficiency, has abundance. *I* is the source of abundance."

It wasn't many hours until another demand came, and I had to pay outward lip service to the situation again by saying, "Be patient; be patient; it will all be taken care of. You know I am not a thief; you be patient and it will be met." Then to myself I had to say, "Oh, no, *I* is God; *I* does not receive anything. *I* is the source; *I* can feed five thousand."

The next day more demands came and the next day and the next day. But with all the appearances against me and having outwardly to deny my Christ-identity by pleading for time or promising to pay, inwardly I stood fast. . . .

It took five days before the first fifty cents came in. It took another week before the trickles of income began to come in. Then gradually a little bit more, a little more, a little bit more, until in a few months harmony was restored. The heavens did not open up and pour down thousand-dollar bills; it came slowly, and it came almost grudgingly, forcing me to acknowledge humanly my lack and inwardly to stand fast in the realization of this truth.[4]

* *I*, italicized, refers to God.

Actually I just had to be a little patient until the first person came and got a healing. From there on it went gradually. One told another, and one told another, and finally a man came in who had such a visible illness that when he was healed within twenty-four hours and there wasn't a sign of it left, many from the church flocked over and from then on I had chairs, not only in my waiting room, but out in the hallway, too. That was the end of waiting. That was the end of lack. That was the end of not being known. . . .

If you sit in the Silence wherever it is, your own will come to you. Sit right down in the middle of the woods and let them beat a pathway to your door. And so it will be, for what God sees in secret is rewarded openly. The state of consciousness that you are is made manifest.[5]

At the end of that year my practice was completely established. It didn't take courage: it took understanding. That is why all my work is conducted without fanfare, without advertising, without promotion.[6]

When Joel moved into an office at 236 Huntington Avenue in Boston, right across the street from The Mother Church, he was the only Christian Science practitioner in the building. For three years he remained the only one there in spite of the fact that his practice was so large that he couldn't take care of it and asked other practitioners to move into the buildng. They were not interested but finally one decided to move in and then a second. Before Joel left that building twenty-three registered practitioners had offices there, and his work had not decreased at all.

There were many times when some of these practitioners met together socially and almost always the conversation centered around the work in which they were all engaged. On one occasion when Joel was talking to three practitioner friends, he expressed his annoyance over the frequent and indiscriminate use of the word "love" by metaphysicians because he maintained that he could not understand it, nor did he feel love. He asked, "What is love? What is the love that I am reading about in the books? How do you love the Lord thy God? How do you love your neighbor as yourself when you do not feel any love?"

They looked at him as if he had lost his mind, protesting that he was one of the most loving persons they knew.

"Me? Oh, don't say anything like that because I must be truthful with you. I do not even feel anything like love. I have no sense of what it means. And truthfully I do not love anybody, and I do not seem to love anything."

"But Joel, you sit up all night to heal somebody and you would go to any lengths to visit a patient; you go to a hospital if there is a need; you do anything that is necessary in the ministry, and that's why we call you loving."

Nevertheless Joel had no sense of being loving or loving anybody. He did all the things his associates thought of as loving for only one reason. It was because he had discovered a principle, and his job was to show it forth, to bring it through, to prove it, not only for the world, but for himself. He could not live with himself unless he proved the principle of the work he was doing. For him, the only love that was involved was the love of this principle, the love of this work, and wanting to see that the whole world caught it.

In the first month of his healing work on one of the occasions when he was having a little talk with God, he promised that he would never refuse any call for help that came to him regardless of where it came from, from whom, what the circumstances were, or what amount of work or labor or anything else was involved in it. He would consider every call for help made to him as if it were coming from God.

It was not long before he was called to visit patients who could not leave their beds or their homes, and within a few years it was taking one whole day a week to drive from place to place to fulfill these demands upon him. Then the work increased so that it took very nearly a second day, and in those two days he was driving over 250 miles every week just calling on those who could not leave their homes.

This phase of the work, he realized, could not continue expanding or he would be frittering away all his time making house calls. That raised certain questions in his mind: Why should that be necessary? What could he do there in the flesh that he could not do sitting quietly in the Spirit? What would be the end of all this if he found that it took seven days a week and more calls came and there were no more days? As he pondered these questions, it became clear to him that he was taking upon himself unnecessary human tasks. He could take on as much of the spiritual activity as was brought to him, but not the human.

Gradually Joel cut down on his visits to patients until in the last ten years of his ministry he made not more than ten calls in all because he had learned that if he sat until he achieved that inner peace and waited for an assurance that God was on the field, the cases were met. To call on a very earnest student who found himself in some kind of difficulty and needed the assurance that Joel was standing by might be an expression of love, not that Joel felt it would be necessary to bring out the healing.

It was during this period that he decided to study Sanskrit so that he could become more familiar with parts of the Hindu Scriptures, and the one place where he could do that was Harvard University. When he applied there, however, he was told that he could not be enrolled in the class because he had no academic background from a recognized educational institution.

I tried to convince them that I had been a reader in a prison service for three years but that didn't seem to constitute institutional background, so I couldn't get in. I wrote a letter to the dean of that department and told him how necessary it was for me to take the course. Incidentally it was a postgraduate course. Without any question, an application form came back with a request for so many dollars, and there I was in Harvard. An eighth grade graduate in Harvard!

At the end of the year, when I asked the dean if I could come back for a second year, he said, "Of course, if you could survive the first year, you can come back for as many as you like. But how did you get here?" He didn't remember allowing me in the course even though I had had no institutional background. But I had an inner drive that had to be satisfied.

Believe it or not, I got to my office at seven o'clock in the morning to begin my healing work, and I went to Harvard at three o'clock in the afternoon and then back to my office. I would work until midnight to make up for lost time, and from midnight until three o'clock in the morning I did my homework. That is a drive. That's not leisure; that's not having money; that's not having somebody to support you. That is drive, and if you have that drive, you can start with one hour that you have now and eventually make room for as many hours as you need. I know these things from personal experience. I know you can do without sleep. I know you can do without food, that is, without a lot of food.[7]

Many interesting experiences came to Joel during his sixteen years as a *Christian Science Journal* practitioner. On one occasion his Christian Science teacher, Charles Heitman, who was a member of the Board of Directors of The Mother Church, asked him for suggestions for a First Reader for The Mother Church, and Joel suggested George Channing.

"But," Mr. Heitman said, "he's been lecturing less than a year and is untried. No one knows his work."

"But I know what he has to offer. He's the only lecturer I go to hear twice in one day." George Channing was appointed, and the attendance at The Mother Church increased noticeably in a few months.

During the time Joel served as First Reader of Third Church of Christ, Scientist, in Boston, it was customary for either the First or Second Reader to introduce the lecturers, and in order to avoid long-drawn-out introductions, the reader was required to submit his introduction in writing to the Board of Directors. In his capacity as First Reader Joel did this, and then one of the Directors of Third Church came to him considerably embarrassed. "You have three paragraphs in your introduction," he said, "and in each paragraph we find incorrect Christian Science. You will have to change it."

"That's easy, but this criticism is more serious than that. If I have written three paragraphs and each one is incorrect, I have no choice. I shall resign at once as Reader and practitioner."

"Oh, no."

"Oh, yes. However, because my teacher is on the Board of The Mother Church, let me submit this to the Directors of The Mother Church."

It was agreed that he should submit his introduction to Mr. Heitman with a letter which said, "This is my introduction for our Christian Science lecturer. Please comment."

Mr. Heitman returned it to Joel in fifteen minutes with the comment, "An excellent job, Joel."

Joel showed it to the Director of Third Church and said, "Now if your Directors and practitioners have any integrity they should all do what I was willing to do, resign." And that ended it.

Joel's experience in the Christian Science movement was a happy and fulfilling one, which he often spoke about not only in private but in public:

The Board of Directors never limited or restricted our activities except in one way. As long as we were listed in the *Journal,* we were not permitted to recommend openly the use of unauthorized literature, but they did not restrict us from reading it. The Directors knew that we were reading the First Edition of our textbook; the Directors knew that we were reading other literature. They knew what we were doing. They weren't blind. They knew that any practitioner who was doing good work had found out some things, and they didn't object to that. They only objected to our confusing our patients by introducing them to things that would bring confusion to them. . . . [8]

And so it was that I watched the Board of Directors in Boston for ten years and I can tell you that they do a magnificent job, a wonderful job with adverse circumstances meeting them every single day of the week. Although they do a lot of things we might not do, nevertheless they are guided by their prayers; they are guided by their intuition; and knowing that about them I appreciate their work.[9]

At some stage of consciousness organization is absolutely necessary to some people. I am one of those who have been deeply blessed by organization. I haven't a word of complaint about it, not a word of criticism, because in my entire experience in organization I was blessed at every step of the way. In fact, I wouldn't take a million dollars in cold cash for my experience in the Christian Science Church. At no time was I oppressed; at no time was my freedom taken from me; at no time was I ever asked to compromise my principles. And so I have nothing but the loudest of praise for organization as I experienced it.

That doesn't mean that everyone experiences the same freedom that I did. Fortunately, I had a very fine Christian Science teacher who blinked his eyes at a lot of things that a lot of other people don't blink their eyes at, and thereby I had a greater degree of freedom. That was my demonstration probably, but the point is this: organization blessed me at that level of consciousness. It couldn't bless me now. Why? Because now I see that it is the activity of truth in consciousness that does this work for me, not whether I go to church on Sunday or Wednesday or give a testimony or whether I get on my knees on Communion Sunday, or whether I do a Daily Lesson. But there are those who need the discipline of organization; there are those who need the coming together in groups, working cooperatively.[10]

I don't know of any more wonderful period of my life than the sixteen years that I was a *Christian Science Journal* practitioner, for I lived morning, noon, and night in the company of those engaged in that church work, and I don't mind telling you they were marvelous people. They didn't all have the full vision. Neither do we all have the full vision. They were living consecrated lives up to the height of their understanding; they were living in and by the Bible. They were living in the Textbook and living by it up to the highest sense of their ability.

That was all I was doing, only up to the highest sense. But what a blessing to come in contact for sixteen years with people who were making a daily study of the Bible, of spiritual writings, spiritual books and magazines, people who were trying to live their lives by demonstration instead of by force! Oh, I count those sixteen years as among my greatest treasures, because they were the preparation for all that followed.[11]

3

Interlude

After ten years in Boston Joel and Rose moved to Florida. Joel was now exceptionally successful in the practice of Christian Science healing, numbering an average of 135 patients a day. Nevertheless he felt that the work could be carried on just as well from Florida or any other place because he had learned that the *I* of him was omnipresent, and therefore, he was not localized in one spot.

They had lived in Florida only a short time when Rose passed away. Joel had been praying for days, praying with all his heart, mind, and soul to save her, and when he was called at three o'clock in the morning to be told that she had gone on, he continued praying until five o'clock, finally going to sleep with a violent headache. When he awakened at nine o'clock the next morning, it was as if Rose appeared to him and said just three words, "Urim and Thummim," which, spiritually interpreted, he understood to mean illumination and the weeding out of personal sense that the disciple might be an instrument for the divine activity.

Twelve hours later, still going through severe pain from the headache brought on through the excitement and stress of the early morning struggle to help Rose, still fighting and arguing with himself that he was able to help other people

but could not help his own wife or himself, and wondering where
this God was that he had relied upon, he again felt the presence of
Rose standing at his side and speaking to him, "Oh, Joel, why don't
you stop that battle? The battle is not yours but God's."

This made him see clearly that the battleground of every problem
is in a person's consciousness, that consciousness is the arena where
the struggle takes place between what we call God, which is good,
and the nonexistent, illusory thing called evil, and that if a person
does not enter into the battle with evil, good will dissolve the illusory appearance of the evil. That quickly was he healed.

Joel told me that Rose studied the Christian Science textbook
twelve hours a day, but inasmuch as her approach was entirely on
the mental level, she could not understand his way of healing. In fact,
she never quite approved of his somewhat unorthodox ideas,
unorthodox, that is, from the standpoint of most metaphysicians.
When she made the transition, however, she evidently saw the cor-
rectness of his teaching and put her seal of approval on it when she
appeared to him after her passing.

The following morning when he awakened he wondered what his
next step should be. Again feeling the presence of Rose, he was led
to the bookcase and opened one of the books to a page where he
read, "In your new consciousness, you will have health and wealth:
health to enjoy wealth, and wealth to enjoy health." Within twenty-
four hours that new consciousness began to take over.

When two friends in New York heard of Rose's passing, they
immediately went down to Florida to be with Joel, and as soon as
they could politely do so, asked him, "What do you expect to do
now?" Joel said that he was going back to practice in Boston as he
had been doing before moving to Florida and that he had already
been able to obtain his former office and an apartment.

It is interesting to note that one of these friends, who had never
given any indication of psychic leanings, turned to him and said,
"No, you are not going to Boston: you are going to California, and
you are going into a new work that is to be widespread and very
successful. Massachusetts won't be able to hold you, and California
won't be big enough either."

Rose and Joel had planned to make a new will so that whoever remained would be taken care of by the considerable estate that had been accumulated. Rose made the transition before this was done, however, and when the estate was being settled, difficulties arose which resulted in a long legal battle. This was the reason for Joel's later admonition never to go into court if it could be avoided by any possible sacrifice. Of this experience Joel said:

> The still small Voice said to me, "Those who live by the sword will die by the sword." It came to me in such a way as to make me understand that I had no right to go to law, not even in this case where I was morally right and where I had been assured, not only by attorneys but by judges, that I was legally right. But instead of taking the word of God, I decided to seek the advice of men, who told me that I was very foolish and was just letting my substance be taken from me.
>
> It did not represent too great a sum of money, but that money was all that I had, so I was convinced by others that it was right to fight for it. But the warning came the second time: "Those who live by the sword will die by the sword. Do not go into court."
>
> My friends, however, prevailed over God. I went into court. . . . I lost the case. . . . It was very sad and pitiful, a hard lesson, but one that I learned.
>
> The law is a fine thing just as armies and navies are fine for those on the level of consciousness where life is lived by might and by power. But to those who come to a higher level of living by the Spirit, it is wrong to use the weapons of the earth. Let us stand clad in the armor of Spirit, and we will never find injustice. I know now that I would not have suffered injustice had I not gone to court. I brought it on myself.[1]

Joel returned to Boston shortly after Rose's passing, and soon thereafter Nellie Steeves, a devoted student, who had been his secretary, called to invite him to Sunday dinner. This invitation he was unable to accept owing to a previous appointment, but it was heartwarming to Joel to have her say to him, "The Steeves' door is always open whenever you can come."

The next day, Sunday, he went to Third Church, and when he met Nellie after the service, he told her that his appointment had been changed and asked her if she still had the roast beef on hand or if she would like to go out for dinner. Nellie, of course, insisted that he have dinner at her home. They had a long talk, and after dinner they went to see her mother, who was in a rest home. Joel then stayed on for the remainder of the afternoon. It could have been that very day when Joel indicated how much he loved Nellie's elderly mother by saying, "Nellie, I can sit in a room with your mother, close my eyes, and reach out and touch God."

Although Nellie was close to Joel during her many years as his secretary, she never knew until some time later when he was giving a talk about supply to a group, that when he returned to Boston from Florida he had only ten dollars in his pocket. It so deeply touched her to think that he would have taken her out to dinner in spite of his empty wallet that she never forgot this example of his total lack of concern about money. He had absolutely no fear of spending his last dollar for dinner or for whatever else the occasion demanded.

Joel was always grateful and appreciative of the work that Nellie Steeves did for him. In fact, at one time he said to me, "It was Nellie Steeves who looked at all the letters I had written to students and patients and said, 'You have material here for a book'; and then she went ahead and helped me get together the book *The Letters.*"[2]

During the past several years I have been in correspondence with Nellie, who has told me many things about Joel in those early days. In June, 1971, she sent me the following letter which Joel wrote her from London on October 14, 1955, eight years after Joel's first book, *The Infinite Way,* had found a goodly measure of success.

Dear Nellie:

Another Infinite Way book (not titled yet) went to the publishers today here in London, a new manuscript. Next week the Dutch translation of *The Infinite Way* will be mailed you from

Holland, and *The Deep Silence* is just translated into Afrikaans. So thought I would celebrate by writing you and sending you a remembrance of your part. All those who now work with me know Nellie Steeves and the work she did, and it has been written into the records of the start of The Infinite Way that you were the very first to work with me, and a record of all you did.

Nellie Steeves is a part of the history of The Infinite Way.

Welcome and Aloha,

Joel

Joel worked hard day and night after his return to Boston, so hard, in fact, that his good friends Dorothy Pendelton and Henry Williams decided that he needed a vacation. They put him on a train bound for California, which seemed the logical place for him to go to escape the rigors of the Boston winter and where he could bask in the sunshine. Actually this marked the end of his Boston days because soon he was involved in teaching spiritual principles in California. Of this move Joel said:

There was a movement from one plane of consciousness to another that outwardly revealed itself by moving from one state to another, but even that was a temporary move because now my home is under my hat, and my hat is somewhere in transit between Hawaii and New York. Evidently the work that has been given me to do could not have been done in Boston, and the farthest place from Boston was California until Hawaii appeared on the scene and now London, Stockholm, and the world.[3]

This move occurred during World War II when apartments were very difficult to find, so he made contact with Nadea Allen, who had been one of Rose's classmates in the Christian Science Class she had taken under Herbert Eustace. Nadea and her mother lived in Santa Monica, and Joel was able to rent rooms on the second floor of their home. Office space, too, was not easy to find. However, he made an arrangement with a Christian Science practitioner, Alex Swan, to use his office in Hollywood from Friday noon until Monday noon while Mr. Swan was at his ranch over the week end.

Later, when Mr. Swan had an accident, Joel was able to give him such excellent help that Alex said to him, "Now I know that you can take care of my practice. For years I have been wanting to go to England to buy cattle for my ranch but I haven't been able to get away from my office."

For nine months Joel used Mr. Swan's office and took care of his practice. When he returned he told Joel that he had done such a good job and his patients were so well satisfied that he had decided Joel should stay and take over his practice, since he had earned it. He would move away and start fresh again.

Joel would have none of that and made it very clear that Alex Swan's practice had come out of his consciousness and no one could take it away from him. They settled the problem by putting up a glass partition and making one office into two. For a whole year they shared this office, and those who came in could get help from whoever was free.

Living in the Allen home in Santa Monica proved to be a pleasant experience. At least once a week on Sunday evenings Nadea invited friends in for supper, during and after which there was much talk of the spiritual way of life. Joel thoroughly enjoyed these soirees and this informal kind of entertaining and conversation. Being with friends who had similar interests always appealed greatly to Joel. He liked visiting and enjoyed recounting the fascinating and sometimes unbelievable experiences life had put in his lap. Always he found himself the center of any gathering as he shared the continuous flow of ideas that kept popping into his head.

In the summer of 1945 he made a quick trip back to Boston to pack up his belongings and send them to California. Just two or three days before he was to return to California, Nellie Steeves' mother fell and broke her wrist and was hospitalized. Nellie called Joel for help, and when she wrote me about this, she said, "Bless his heart, he offered to delay his trip as he thought Mother and I would feel better if he were standing by." Of course, Nellie refused to permit him to do this, telling him that he could help her mother in California just as well as in Boston, which proved to be true. This is another example of that love that Joel said he never felt but which he demonstrated so clearly and poured out so freely.

About this time Joel and Nadea decided to be married. It seemed an ideal arrangement, since both of them were in the healing practice and devoted to the spiritual life.

The night before their marriage a friend gave Joel a chain reference Bible which he scanned with great interest, especially certain passages of Paul's on immortality which challenged his attention. He put the Bible in his bag to take with him the next day when they left for their honeymoon after a simple marriage ceremony. The minute they arrived at their hotel in Desert Hot Springs, he said to his bride, "Let me get at this book right away." That day and that night Joel wrote feverishly, with Nadea encouraging him, and the first chapter of *The Infinite Way* took form.

For some time Joel had pondered over the limitations that he felt resulted from organization, and as the work on *The Infinite Way* progressed, he decided that in order to be free to follow the way that was revealing itself to him he should sever his ties with organized activities and proceed alone. Consequently he withdrew from the Christian Science Church, gave up the office which he had shared with Alex Swan and set out to publish *The Infinite Way*. He had only two thousand copies printed, because he did not think the book would be taken seriously by anybody but a few friends and patients to whom he thought he might possibly give five hundred copies. The other fifteen hundred were stored in the garage of their new home on Sierra Bonita Avenue in Hollywood with no idea of what to do with them.

Since Joel had separated himself from the Christian Science movement before publishing his first book, he was convinced that this marked the end of his active career. He often said that he expected to spend the rest of his days in California doing a little healing work and staying quietly at home with Nadea, enjoying the good California weather. He envisioned a beautiful office in Hollywood where he would go every day about nine o'clock and stay until four or five and where people could drop in who were seeking healing.

Then if some of them wanted to buy the little book, they could learn how it happened.

This whole period of his life was a very happy one. Practically every day for luncheon he went over to the Farmers' Market for a salad and some iced tea. In the winter Nadea and he went down to Desert Hot Springs or Palm Springs for the week end and in the summer they would go up to Santa Barbara.

This semiretirement was of short duration, however. It was soon broken when a mother, father, and son drove out to California from Ohio and asked Joel to give them class instruction.

"That's impossible," he said, "I'm not a teacher."

"Well, but you are not in Christian Science now, so you can teach if you want to, in fact, do whatever you want to do."

"How can you teach if you're not a teacher, whether you are in or out? And I am not a teacher."

"Well, we are here because we think that you know something that we want to know."

"Can't imagine what it is."

At last Joel agreed that since they had made the trip he would work with them in his home every night for two weeks as best he could. This he did. When they left they were very appreciative, felt that Joel had given them a great deal, and left him a check for an amount which would have covered the class instruction fee for the three in a Christian Science class. It was a mystery to Joel why they had sought him out. He could not understand it, but he thought it was because they were good friends of his.

A few days later four couples came and asked him if he would teach them the Bible, to which Joel replied that he could not teach them anything about the Bible because he understood exactly two statements in it and knew nothing of its history and background. For two weeks, however, they gave him no rest, telling him that they knew that he must know something that he had not told them. Finally he decided that the only way to end this would be for them to come one night a week for four weeks, and by that time they would understand that he did not know enough about the Bible to teach them. That is the way they began.

A few days before that first Friday night Joel went to his office and spoke to God: "Look, Father, if You sent these people to me, it must be for a reason. Tell me what it is. If You didn't send them, that's all right. Within four weeks, they will know all about it, but if You sent them, let me in on the secret. What are they here for? What is it You want me to do?"

I talked to the Father as if the Father were another man. That isn't very metaphysical, but that is my way, and that is the way I still talk to the Father. So I sat with the Bible in my hand, waited, waited, and waited, and finally I opened it and found myself reading something about Moses. Now if there ever was a mystery to me, it was the man Moses and the flight out of Egypt and across the desert with forty years of travel. So as I was reading that, I thought that I might as well go back to the beginning of the account of Moses and read it all the way through. This I did.

When we met on the first Friday, there were four married couples who came to my home. They were very much shocked when I told them that the ministry of Moses was a human ministry, leading ignorance, superstition, and illiteracy out of itself into a preparation for something better. That is why Moses did not enter the Promised Land. Good humanhood will never take a person into the Promised Land. Good humanhood is a preparation for it, but then your teacher who told you about being good has to leave you, and the spiritual one has to come along to lift you into divine Consciousness. That was the subject of the first lesson.

Three of those couples thought it was wonderful, but the other couple thought it was shocking and dropped out. The next Friday night, however, because of what they had heard from the first three, four new couples took the place of the one couple who had dropped out. Before that Friday night I went back to the Father and said, "Where do we go from here? It was You that started me off last week. I think You did all right, and You must have something for me this week, too."

When I opened the Bible, it was to the book of Ruth. I had read the story of Ruth and Naomi many times and appreciated the beauty of the passage, "Entreat me not to leave thee," but I could not see the spiritual message in it. I read it over several times, and then all of a sudden its meaning dawned on me.[4]

After the fourth week it was decided to continue the class for another six weeks. Thirty-two people were now meeting together and that was all the room would hold. In order to take care of the students who wanted to participate in this work, he began holding classes two nights of the week. Then it was necessary to move to an office that held fifty persons, and the meetings were extended to three nights a week. Finally fifty people were meeting five nights a week in an office, and another group two nights a week either in San Francisco or down on the desert. With each of these meetings there came an unfoldment of some passage or some story from the Bible, and, through this, Joel himself was learning about the Bible. For sixty weeks the class continued, and then some of the students asked for a summation of the work in written form.

Several members of the class who had taken notes gave them to Joel, and out of their notes came the book *Spiritual Interpretation of Scripture.*[5] This book was never a book written by an author: it was the fruitage of meditation brought to light.

One step followed another. Ernest Holmes invited Joel to speak at the Science of Mind Center, where, as usual, Joel did not present orthodox metaphysics, instead giving out the truth as he saw it. So, without thinking, because he never planned what he was going to say in advance, out came the shattering statement: "One of the basic principles of The Infinite Way is that thought is not power."

The audience reacted as if a ton of bricks had hit them. Two women jumped up immediately after the meeting and came up to him, saying, "You told us tonight that thought is not power, and here we have come all the way from New York to California to learn how to use the power of thought."

"Well," Joel said, "when you succeed, I don't suppose you would have any objection to money, as long as you get it honestly?"

"No, of course not."

"You can take back about a million dollars to your husbands. California is really a paradise. California has the most perfect of everything except for one little fault. It doesn't rain here all summer. Things get dry, so as soon as you learn how to use the power of thought, for heaven's sake give us some rain. There's a fortune waiting here for you."

Being the forthright person that he was, this was typical of Joel. He could be very tactless and abrupt, and certainly he never made any attempt to curry favor with people or to draw them to him.

Some of the Bible lessons had been given in San Francisco, so now he found himself invited there to give lectures and classes. Students felt that the things Joel was saying should be recorded on a wire recorder and then distributed in typewritten form so that they would be able to go over them again, read, study, and bring them back to their remembrance. Joel was reluctant to have this done because he felt he was not saying anything that was particularly important or worthwhile. The students were sufficiently persuasive, however, so he consented on the condition that if he did not like the result of their work, it would be destroyed.

As soon as a class session was over, a secretary sat up all night to make a transcript of the material, which she gave to Joel at four o'clock in the morning. When he read it, he could not believe that he had said some of those things, but he was told that all he would have to do to verify the transcript was to listen to the recording. He thereupon corrected the transcript, and by two o'clock the following afternoon it was ready to be mimeographed. Then came pressure on him to have the notes of the entire class assembled into a book. He asked how much it would cost to do this, and when he was told that it would be $7.50 a copy, he said that nobody would pay that for it. Nevertheless it was done, and although there were only sixty-six students in the class, one hundred copies were sold. This mimeographed paper-covered volume was entitled *Metaphysical Notes.*[6]

During this class in San Francisco Joel experienced what he considered one of the most sacred nights that had ever happened to him in all his work.

My wife came up for a few days for the close of the class, and that night I retired and evidently went to sleep. Along about three o'clock in the morning I was awakened, and an inner urge told me to get out of bed. As I did so and sat up in a chair, I was flooded with a message. I sat there and listened to every word of it. Never had I heard such words. Never had such a message come through me before. It held me spellbound. I didn't think it up: I heard it. I felt it coming through.

My wife awakened and wanted to know what I was doing, and I said, "You just lie there quietly. Something is coming." As she had had that experience with me before, she knew enough to be still.

After this, came the Voice that said to me, "Now write it down." I went to the desk and wrote as it came again word for word, slowly enough so that I could write it. Then It said, "Give this to the class tonight," and this is the message that is called "Ordination" in *Conscious Union with God.*

When I had finished writing, I can hardly tell you what happened. All I know is that I began to cry, and Nadea told me that the stirring within that came with that ordination lasted until six o'clock in the morning. Why? After a person has been talking, contemplating, and thinking about God continuously, he gets into a depth of meditation where he touches the place that Jesus called the kingdom of God, the realm of God within. Then it begins to unfold and reveal itself as an inner communion, but it takes him so completely out of this world that sometimes on coming back into the world, there may be that period of weeping and crying.

That night when I gave the lesson on Ordination to the class there was a stillness that could have been cut with a knife. I couldn't speak afterwards, and nobody even wanted to hear anything more, so we just remained quiet for a few minutes and everyone filed out and went home, with not a word spoken.[7]

When Joel read that message again years afterwards, he could still feel that quickening of the Spirit from head to foot, remembering the experience during which it was given to him twice in one night.

After that Joel was invited to go to Portland, Oregon, to address a healing conference, and then received invitations to go to Victoria and Vancouver, B. C., and Seattle, Washington. While he was in Portland in 1951, Mrs. Nellie Kloh, who was in charge of a metaphysical center there, asked if he would permit her to have the class and lecture work recorded on a tape recorder. At that time Joel had never heard of a tape recorder, but he consented, and it was there that the tape recording work which was to be such an important factor in the spread of the message began, with Joel greatly opposed to every step of it.

During this period, by a curious set of circumstances, Joel was called to Hawaii. The chain of events began in 1950 when Joel was driving to Los Angeles after some work he had done in San Francisco. While he was going through San Luis Obispo, he heard within himself these words: "God performeth that which is given me to do." He could not recall ever having consciously heard them before and did not know where they came from, but to him the words sounded like a passage from Scripture. After he had heard them repeated two or three times, he pulled up alongside the road and looked in the concordance of the Bible he always carried with him. He found these two verses: "He performeth the thing that is appointed for me," and "He perfecteth that which concerneth me." It was an enigma to him why these two passages should come to him at this time, but all he could say was, "Thank You, Father; just bring it along and let me have it. As long as You are going to do it, I have no fear."

When he arrived home in Los Angeles, Nadea said, "Dinner will be ready in about twenty minutes so just wait in your study." As he sat down in his study, the telephone rang. It was Hawaii, a friend who with great urgency in her voice asked, "Can you come to Honolulu? My husband is ill, and the doctors have said that he can't live this week out."

"Yes, I can come. I have just finished a class, and I have some weeks ahead of me without having made any arrangements for the next work. I will be glad to come, but remember that your husband's healing is not dependent on my coming. I will get to work right away. What about transportation? How do I get there?"

"Oh," she said, "we'll take care of that. You will have a call."

A couple of days later the telephone rang with news that his ticket was awaiting him in San Francisco, and he was to sail Saturday for Honolulu. Then the doorbell rang and there was an airmail special delivery letter from a couple on the Island of Maui, saying, "We have just discovered your writings out here and think they are wonderful. Do you ever come to Hawaii? We would like some instruction." Joel cabled immediately that he was sailing on Saturday for Honolulu.

When he arrived, the friend who had first telephoned him met him at the ship with her husband, now completely recovered from his illness. Then at the hotel he received a telephone call that the couple from Maui were registered there and waiting to see him.

It was not long afterward that Joel received an invitation to give a series of talks at the Unity Center in Waikiki, Honolulu. There he met Emma Lindsay, a beautiful woman, slender, with soft brown hair and large blue eyes that could become warm or cold, depending upon whom they rested. Actually he did not meet Emma first but her six-year-old son Sam, who came to place a lei on Joel at this meeting. With true Hawaiian hospitality Emma asked Joel if he would like to take a drive around the island, and, having a little free time, he accepted with pleasure. From then on they saw each other often during his visit at that time and also on his subsequent trips to Hawaii.

Emma was working as a bookkeeper at a world-famous beauty salon and boutique in Honolulu, and living with her daughter Geri and son-in-law Lieutenant Commander Jack McDonald. Not long after meeting Joel she became interested in helping him make tape recordings on a very simple and unprofessional scale and soon left the salon to devote her entire time to that activity. At first there was not even a connection from one tape recorder to the other, so Emma simply played the recording on one tape recorder and let the other pick it up through the microphone, together with all the noise from outside and inside caught on the recording—a time-consuming and often frustrating undertaking at which she worked tirelessly and with great devotion. To Joel, life in Hawaii became more and more appealing. He liked the climate, the pure air, the quiet, and his daily swim in the Pacific, so after several trips to Hawaii he decided to make his home there permanently. He asked Nadea to go with him, but for a number of reasons she seemed unwilling to move to the Islands. Thus the relationship between Joel and Nadea became increasingly strained. While Nadea appreciated and encouraged Joel in the work he was doing, she remained loyal to Christian Science and her teacher and was either unwilling or unable to go along with Joel in this new dimension in which he found himself. Friction increased to the point of no return. When Nadea continued to refuse to make the move to Honolulu, Joel finally asked for a divorce, which led to considerable hard feelings and a great deal of misunderstanding. Those who knew and loved them both began to take sides, and the lines were sharply drawn.

Several years passed before the divorce was granted, but on January 16, 1956, Joel wrote me from Kailua:

> Divorce granted Jan. 10—and all payments have been completed. Was able to pay every cent, and now have only a monthly payment . . . to make.

Joel always recognized his great debt to Nadea. It was in her home that The Infinite Way was born, and he felt that she had been largely responsible for encouraging him to go ahead and write the book *The Infinite Way.* Strange that the very thing she wanted him to do was the thing that eventually separated them! Joel often told me how she worked indefatigably, distributing his early writings and keeping in touch with those who were interested in the work. She was a warm and vital woman, highly intelligent and alert, and an excellent practitioner, so excellent that whenever Joel had a severe migraine headache—and they came to him on occasion—Nadea could snap him out of it instantaneously. To her, every such thing was mental malpractice.

Joel had wanted very much to have Nadea travel with him wherever he went, but this she could not or would not do, perhaps partly because she felt she could not leave her mother, who was advanced in years, and who after breaking her hip could not be left alone. Furthermore Nadea was tied to old allegiances and old patterns of thinking, and no matter how much Joel longed to be able to take the one closest to him with him on his human journey and much more so on his spiritual journey, it was not to be. So Joel continued as the lone traveler.

4

Initiation

In his sixteen years of healing work the Bible, for the most part, had been a closed book to Joel. He read it; he was familiar with many passages that were in it; but, as he explained to those first students who persuaded him to teach them the Bible, there were only two statements that he could truthfully say he understood. One was from Isaiah: "Cease ye from man, whose breath is in his nostrils: for wherein is he to be accounted of." He caught a vision of what that meant, and that was enough to make his practice flourish. Joel spent eight months with that one statement until its companion statement came to him from the book of John in the New Testament: "My kingdom is not of this world."

Out of those two statements came the whole message of The Infinite Way, and while there were many other passages and some poetry in the Bible that Joel liked very much, they had little actual meaning or attraction for him. Those two statements, however, were always present in his consciousness.

Every day people were coming to him for healing, and he had to do one of two things: try to heal them or forget them. Scripture says, "Cease ye from man," meaning forget man, let the human being go, drop him out of consciousness: do not try to heal him; do not try to reform him; do not try to enrich him. Look through the masquerade and behold the Christ. Can you imagine a man, sitting in a busy office with a busy practice, people of all kinds and with all sorts of things of this world coming to him, and having to say to them, "My kingdom is not of this world," which really meant that he was not interested in their problems? But Joel had caught a glimpse of the spiritual kingdom and knew that there was no use in trying to patch up a human world or a human body. What was necessary was to rise into a new dimension of consciousness.

As early as 1932 it had become clear to Joel that meditation was the way, and he began an earnest search to discover the secret. The few books he found on the subject, some from the Occident and some from the Orient, he read with avidity but none gave him what he was seeking.

One day the idea came to him that he should sit in quiet and silence and see what would happen. He did this and nothing happened. Later that same day he tried it again with the same lack of results.

Finally, he was at the point where he was sitting quietly in silence eight times a day, from two to five minutes each time, trying to meditate, but still nothing whatsoever happened, that is, nothing of which he was aware. It was only after eight months that he felt what he described as the "click," no sound as such, but a pulling in, a deep breath, and he knew then that something of a different nature had happened. That day, the rest of his morning was more harmonious and peaceful, more successful than what he had known previously. It seemed to wear off, however, before noontime, and he tried several times during the afternoon to re-create that morning's experience and renew it, but without success.

A number of days went by before he achieved that sense of the "click" again. Eventually, the experience came twice in one day out of eight or ten attempts. When it did come, even though it was nothing more than a deep beeath, it changed his day. The harmony in his relationship with others began to improve and there was a noticeable increase in his income. As far back as 1933 he had been meditating some part of every hour of the day and most of the hours of the night, which resulted in his sleeping only three and a half hours out of the twenty-four. He continued to maintain his practice, did a vast amount of reading, and at the same time attended Harvard University studying Sanskrit.

Sitting at his desk in 1934, a startling message came to him out of the nowhere: thought is not power. It was startling to him because that was the era when the idea that thought is power was sweeping the country, and not only that, some persons were beginning to believe that thought was the real power and the only power. And then here came this disquieting unfoldment: thought is not power.

This was as upsetting to him as must have been the revelation centuries ago, to those entrenched in the old belief of a flat world, that the earth was round. Inside he churned; inside he was disturbed; inside a revolution was going on. Thought is not power in this age when so many teachings are dedicated to that very idea? Isn't thought power? Isn't thought all power? Doesn't thought govern? It took days and days of meditation, days and days of pondering to learn whether he was being deceived from inside or whether something of an important nature was coming through.

But Joel had ample opportunity to prove how ineffectual thought can be. He learned that thought might serve to lift a person to a place of stillness, but he knew that when a person is up against a really serious problem, there is not a thought anywhere that will really help. Only the *realization* of God can bring harmony into such a situation. It is not the form of prayer that brings the miracle of Grace that appears as healing; it is not the truth that a person knows: it is the Spirit that becomes active in consciousness. If It is active, It will raise up edifices; It will raise up dead bodies. "If you destroy this body, in three days, I," this Christ, "will raise it up again."

Of this period, when Joel sat in a practitioner's office doing healing work from morning until night, six days a week, he wrote:

> For sixteen years, I lived between two worlds, outwardly as a healer, living a normal family life, inwardly apart from "this world," as if I had already departed it. All these years were

unhappy ones for the outer man, and probably for the family also, and inwardly a sensationless life of learning. Secrets of the Orient and the Occident were revealed to me, secrets of the mind of man and of the spiritual realm. Laws of mind and the grace of Spirit revealed themselves to me.

I have never minded the misery of my personal life, only the unhappiness of those who touched my outer life and couldn't enter into the inner with me. Never having experienced either the victories or the defeats of human existence, it was a complete transition to the life of the Spirit.

It is not a pleasant experience to witness neophytes seeking the spiritual way, because they are looking so eagerly to imagined joys, successes, and honors, and these I have never found. Why, then, the spiritual life? It is given to those who receive it for some special purpose of the inner Realm, and not for an individual's triumphant life. It is given by an act of Grace for a mission; and as one's life is not one's own, there can be no victories, no profits, no satisfaction of any personal nature. Those who receive ordination are fortunate that they are called to serve, but they must remember that it is not for their benefit or glory, but that a work be accomplished.

Think, neophytes, before you knock seriously. Think! You will live in two worlds, in this world but not of it. Your standards, your emotions, your words, and your ways will not be of "this world," and so you will be alienated from your friends and family and community, and yet compelled to live and work among them. You will meet only a few of your own household, and these seldom, and each will be fully occupied with his own mission. Your relationship with those of the world will be unsatisfactory; your periods of peace only when in inner contemplation and communion.[1]

As he became more adept at meditation, more spiritual experiences began to come, and these increased until in 1945 an impartation from within told him in no uncertain terms, "Next year is your year of transition."

I didn't like that. That sounded to me too much like dying or passing on, and I had long since agreed that I liked life well enough to stay here for about two hundred years and then decide whether I would like to continue a little longer. Here I was being told by the Voice that I had learned to trust that next year was to be my year of transition. When I protested about it, the Voice came right back and said, "Not that kind of transition. This is a transition into a different state of consciousness."[2]

Joel was devoting his full time to healing work and teaching what he had learned of the nature of God and prayer to individuals who came to him, but more particularly teaching meditation. As those who came to him learned how to meditate, they were able to make an inner contact, and then they had no further need to go back to him except for the joy of spiritual communion and of further meditation with him.

In 1946, the year after I was told that that would be my year of transition, a member of my family said that for several days I had eaten no meat and asked if that was intentional and if there were any reason for it. It was the first that I was aware of it. Evidently it had been an unconscious act. Within a day or two after that, however, in July, the spiritual experience of initiation began and lasted for two months.[3]

Every morning at five o'clock I was awakened and made to sit in a chair until seven o'clock, two solid hours. Every day I went through an inner illumination that seemed to open my consciousness, and it was as if I were witnessing the equivalent of a Masonic initiation. It seemed that I was witnessing an awesome ceremony and being initiated into spiritual truth. I considered this the first illumination which was a revelation of something I could specifically grasp hold of and say, "Now, I know what this is and I can tell it." And that was the year in which *The Infinite Way* was completed.

It was the most beautiful two months of my entire life, and at the end of that time I was told in very plain words, "From now on you will teach, but you will never seek a student. You will accept those students who are led to you. You will never need anything, but you will let transpire whatever transpires."[4]

From one of Joel's personal notes that he sent me in January, 1964, but which he had written many years before, he gave further information about what he learned during this initiation:

"The prayer of a righteous man availeth much." Heretofore we have sought to have God purify us. We have waited for some visitation from without or from within, which should miraculously cleanse us, purge us, and eventually forgive us our sins.

In my own initiation and purification, I learned this: We ourselves must initiate the steps necessary to the unfoldment of God within and to His government of our lives.

In 1957 Joel told me that when he visited the Parthenon in Athens in 1955 he found it strangely familiar because it seemed to him to have been the exact place where his initiation had come about in those early morning hours in Santa Monica in 1946.

That was not the only initiation he experienced, however. There were many in the years that followed, but for the most part he was reluctant to share any of these beyond what is recorded here.

Experienced an initiation Saturday morning, brief but powerful. So far, no relation to the class.[5]

Today I received a new ordination. Following are the notes: . . . Told: "Be separate. Live *in* the world but not *of* it. The Spirit of God is in you (indeed it is). You will live in two worlds—in the spiritual world learning of Its ways, and by Its grace expressing in the human world. *My* Spirit is upon you. Hear, speak, live through *My* Spirit. *My* grace is the strength, knowledge, support, supply, for all your work."

To me was shown the lotus of purity, the lily of immortality —signs of the presence of the Spirit.

And so it is.[6]

Joel maintained that there are many fictional accounts of initiation repeated by novelists and other people, reporting something that they heard somebody say in Egypt, India, or Tibet, but to his knowledge nowhere on earth was there a record of a revelation by a master of what had made him a master. He was sure that Jesus never gave the secrets of his initiation even to his disciples.

Before the completion of *The Infinite Way* Joel was given a vision of the past, the present, and the future. In that vision he transcended time and space, and the whole of life was revealed in the magnitude of this experience. *The Infinite Way* was not something that just happened. It was the fruitage of all his years of study and practice, the fruitage of that unswerving dedication to principle which finally came to a head in this book.

Long before that, while he was First Reader of Third Church of Christ, Scientist, in Boston, sitting at his desk on November 20, 1940, at 1:45 P.M. he wrote, "My task will be to gather those around me who understand truth as it is presented in my writings." At that time there were no students and there were no writings, but he set this down in writing and never saw it again until 1946 when he was going through some of his papers. It was a forecast of future events, but must have seemed strange to him at that time.

Then, in Santa Monica, California, when the manuscript of *The Infinite Way* was just coming into form, he found another bit of writing evidently from the same pad, dated 1937:

Illumination dissolves all material ties and binds men together with the golden chains of spiritual understanding; it acknowledges only the leadership of the Christ; it has no ritual or rule but the divine, impersonal universal Love; no other worship than the inner Flame that is ever lit at the shrine of Spirit. This union is the free state of spiritual brotherhood. The only restraint is the discipline of Soul, therefore we know liberty without license; we are a united universe without physical limits; a divine service to God without ceremony or creed. The illumined walk without fear—by Grace.[7]

Of this passage Joel spoke later in wonder:

> How does a Christian Science practitioner ever write a thing like that? How could I ever dream of such a thing as breaking material ties or of a spiritual brotherhood or of a united service to God? Thoughts such as these do not enter one's mind unless they come out of the Universal. It was written in 1937, and I never saw it again until 1946, and here it crops up three thousand miles away. I didn't understand it, but I liked it and so I put it in on page forty of *The Infinite Way.*
>
> As the book was ready for press, the same passage came to my mind again, and I said to the publisher, "I want that passage put in the front of every book, of every manuscript, or every pamphlet that may ever appear with my name on it."[8]

Even then Joel did not know why this was so significant because he had no idea of the work that lay ahead of him. Later he said that the same Thing that gave him that message in 1937 wrote *The Infinite Way* and provided the cue for the whole of Infinite Way work throughout all time.

From the earliest days of Joel's healing ministry he wrote letters to his patients, sometimes voluminous ones. Soon, he found himself writing a weekly letter to those who wanted a message of truth from him, and although some of these letters went into the book *The Infinite Way,* several of the chapters were written specifically for the book, such as the first chapter on "Immortality," the chapter on "Supply," and the one entitled "The New Horizon," which Joel recognized as the most important chapter in the whole book. And it came out of a dream.

In his entire lifetime, according to Joel, he had probably had not more than a hundred dreams, and all but one of them were nonsensical. But this one dream had real significance for him and gave him the chapter "The New Horizon."

One night in Santa Monica while he was in a deep sleep, a red silk banner was lowered from the ceiling. On it was a message in Old English gold lettering, and although he was dreaming, he knew that it was a dream. He also knew that he had to awaken to write down what he saw, and so he forced himself awake. Even when he was awake, the banner was still there, and he wrote down the message that was on that banner. When he had finished, the banner rolled itself up and disappeared.

The next morning Joel gave a copy of what he had written to his secretary, Nellie Steeves, who had moved to California. Her response was, "Oh, that's the last chapter of the book." While it is not the last chapter, it is one of the last, and Joel always felt that it is one of the most important in his writings because it brings out so clearly that before a person can enter into the spiritual life, not only the bad of human experience must be given up but the good also. Many times I have heard Joel ask students to read nothing but that chapter for two weeks or a month, and to contemplate its meaning.

The chapter on "Supply" in *The Infinite Way* had such an impact on those who read it that it was finally printed in pamphlet form. While this was a subject on which Joel could speak with authority because he had worked through that problem in his own early experience of lack, he had always thought that it was a subject that could not be explained in words alone.

One day, however, when he and his wife were driving from Los Angeles to the desert, they passed through a citrus grove area where oranges, grapefruit, and lemons were growing. It was at that moment that he was given such an insight into the subject of supply that he felt he could teach it to those who were unfamiliar with the vision he had had on the nature of supply as not anything that is visible but as that which flows forth out of the consciousness of individual being. As the method of presentation of the subject of supply unfolded to him, using the orange and the orange tree as an example, he enthusiastically told it to Nadea. She with equal enthusiasm told him to be sure to write it down because this was really it. And so it was that the chapter on supply was born.

When *The Infinite Way* was to be published, Joel sent it to practically every large publisher in New York City. Some read it once and some twice, but all passed it up as a book that would have no appeal. Eventually, Joel had it published in Los Angeles and paid for the cost of publication himself. There seemed to be little appreciation in the United States for a book that was ultimately to have such a profound effect on the lives of so many people.

Three or four years later someone sent a copy of *The Infinite Way* to Henry Thomas Hamblin in England. When Mr. Hamblin read it, he wrote to Joel, "This is what I have been waiting for and this is what the world is waiting for. This is the teaching of Jesus Christ on earth again." He wrote an article on *The Infinite Way* which was published in his *Science of Thought* magazine, with the result that the publishers, George Allen and Unwin, Ltd., of London, asked Joel for permission to publish it in a British edition.

Joel's years of meditating—the years of study, the years of one-pointed dedication to the living of the principles which became clearer and clearer—had culminated in the two months of inner initiation which stripped aside every veil. Then the full revelation of the principles of spiritual living and healing were given him. To prove the validity of these principles he devoted the remaining years of his life.

His initiation lifted him completely out of the realm of metaphysics into pure mysticism. The metaphysics Joel had lived with for so many years but which he had never fully accepted remained a part of his background and constituted the skeletal foundation on which the mystical revelation was built.

Joel's mysticism did not consist primarily in phenomenal experiences: seeing lights or living on visions, although as a visionary he did penetrate beyond what the world sees to that unknown realm that is here and now but is unperceived by the gross physical senses. His visions and the Voice of which he spoke so frequently came to him as impartations, impressions from within.

> I am not alone in this work. There is a Spirit that has been with me since my first illumination, and it is not a person as far as I know. I do not hear voices dictating messages or anything of that kind. But there is this Spirit, a Presence, which I feel sometimes here, sometimes sitting on my shoulder.
>
> This Spirit has always been with me in my work. This Spirit

is my life, the harmony of my being, my supply. I have not had to take human footsteps for supply because it has always come, although at first slowly.

This Spirit has carried this message around the whole world and has kept me in health. I have had only one serious illness in thirty years, and yet I work hard—for twenty of those years, twenty hours a day with three and a half hours of sleep. And even today I still work hard answering my mail, doing the healing work, the teaching, lecturing, and traveling, living in hotels. But I am not fatigued; I am not run down; I am not weary; I am not played out because this is the Spirit. It isn't my health: it's that Spirit that keeps me going, and that is what has given me this work ever since 1928 in the month of November. It has always been with me, always.[9]

Joel Goldsmith can rightly be called a mystic because he attained conscious oneness with the Source of all life. In those moments of soaring consciousness in which he lived much of the time, there was no veil between him and ultimate Reality because there was no twoness. He saw the "new heaven and new earth" as here and now and recognized human experience with its good and evil as mesmeric suggestion, stemming from the world belief in two powers into which every human being is born.

5

🪷 No Longer the Lone Traveler

The interlude in California was a fruitful one, during which Joel experienced the initiation that brought The Infinite Way into focus. In many ways they were pleasant years, years of expanding awareness in which step by step he was taken further and further away from metaphysics into mysticism.

Yet they were years of great inner turmoil. Joel's own notations are clear-cut evidence of this. But with all the turmoil, the inner unfoldments of this period were rich and pregnant with meaning for the future of The Infinite Way. This inner unfoldment which continued throughout his earthly experience is shown in some of his early notations, jotted down as they came to him. They indicate the spiritual heights to which he ascended as well as the torment of a soul that had glimpsed a vision beyond this world, but was unable to maintain it every moment, and therefore experienced the pain of being in the world while catching a vision of life lived wholly in that Kingdom which is not of this world.

The gentle breezes, the warmth, and the beauty of Hawaii struck a responsive chord in Joel. There he could feel the ryhthm of the universe as he watched the Southern

Cross move silently across the heavens, listened to the ebb and flow of the waves as they dashed upon the shore, and heard the quiet rustle of the palms. All this made him more conscious than ever before of a divine law in operation. There he could feel the pulsating life force of the universe. Hawaii had really taken hold of him, and after he had decided to make his home there permanently, he left California, returned to Honolulu, and lived for a time at the Halekulani Hotel, later taking an apartment on the Ala-wai.

Wherever Joel went a group of students gathered around him, with Emma Lindsay almost always present. Another person who also had a great deal of contact with Joel in those days was Floyd Nowell, a building contractor who for a time was one of Joel's most devoted students. When they first met, he was having a difficult time with his business, but his work with Joel quickly changed that, and he soon found himself very successful.

It was Floyd and Emma who told Joel, "You should have a home where students could come to visit you and be taught when they felt the need, and it should be where you would have a maximum of comfort."

Joel's answer was a natural and normal one when considered out of his past experience: "Well, if the time ever comes when there is a legitimate need for that, I am sure the students will provide it, and I will be there."

With that the subject was dropped, but in the middle of the night Joel awakened out of a sleep, and the Voice said to him, "You taught them incorrectly."

"What?"

"Oh, yes, you taught them incorrectly."

He wondered what this meant and what was incorrect about what he had taught them. He went back to that afternoon and kept thinking about it until it came to him: "Why, you are the teacher. You are to show forth the bounties and the abundance of the Father, and you are expecting the students to provide for the teacher who is supposed to feed the multitudes. If they provided for you, they would be the teacher, and you would be the student. If you are teaching the infinite nature of Spirit, prove it to them. And if there is a need for this, show them that the Spirit provides all things, and that they can go and do likewise."

Not long after that he purchased a modest little house at 22 Kailua Road in Kailua, about a mile from the house that Emma had purchased, and where a studio had been built for the tape recording work. After the purchase and his move to his new home on February 11, 1955, he settled in like a good householder and made arrangements for whatever changes were necessary from time to time.

> Had my Venetian blinds taken down and replaced with bamboo poinciana drapes; having lower windows put in bath and kitchen; had floors done today—triple waxing, as all my floors are asphalt tile; am getting in a dishwasher; and having library shelves (I mean bookshelves) built in office and bedroom for the overflow. So house is about complete.[1]

During the period when Joel was spending most of his time in Hawaii, even while he still maintained a home in California, the work continued to flourish. He gave *The 1952 First Honolulu Closed Class* and two years later *The 1954 Honolulu Closed Class* and also a class for practitioners. In addition to that, there were a number of classes on the mainland, a trip to England and the Continent in late 1953 and early January, 1954, and in 1954 he carried the message around the world. But always he traveled alone.

Emma worked tirelessly for Joel. Every day she left her home to look after his house, do his marketing, prepare his meals when they did not eat out, and chauffeured students, who came from all over the world, across the Pali from Waikiki to Kailua, a distance of about fifteen miles each way over roads not too good in those early days. After all these things were taken care of, she sometimes worked into the early hours of the morning, making the tape recordings in her home and keeping all the accounts, including subscriptions that came in for the monthly *Letter*.

While I had had some correspondence with Emma in regard to the tapes, I did not meet her until March, 1956, when she accompanied Joel to New York to tape record the classes during the month of classwork held there. One morning four of us had breakfast together

—Joel, Emma, another student, and I. This was my first opportunity to sit down and talk with Emma face to face, and gave me some insight into her as a person. The conversation turned to the subject of the little luxuries of life, and I guiltily confessed that I still enjoyed beautiful china, silver, and linens. It came as a great surprise to me when they almost unanimously said, "We do, too." Emma went on to mention some of the lovely things that she enjoyed having in her home. The fact that these people, too, enjoyed some of the pleasures and comforts of this world and did not live as ascetics was reassuring to me. As usual, Joel used this opportunity to point up the principle that the spiritual life should show forth as a greater appreciation of beauty, although with no sense of desire or possession.

As far back as 1954 Joel had said to me, "When I have a little quiet time, we will go deep into the work, and you will come to Hawaii for that." So in 1957 Joel invited me to come to Hawaii to work with him, ordered an airplane ticket for me, and sent the following letter on January 15, 1957;

> Have arranged your Hawaii home, and The Infinite Way will pay for it while you are here: a large room, refrigerator, range, and bath in Waikiki. The manager is one of our students, and you will find our books, tapes, and recorder all over the place—like home! . . . .
>
> We will be at the plane. Cable any change of plans to Honolulu.

On January 25, 1957, he wrote the following letter to my sister Valborg, who was at that time living in Washington, D. C.:

> It is Friday evening, so just two nights and Lorraine will be here. Be assured that we will see that she does not have to sleep in the snow or stand in the breadline. Even out here in Tropic Land we have Serta mattresses, electric refrigerators, refrigeration, and American food. Yes, Lorraine will be given Hawaiian hospitality. Her hotel is managed by one of our students, has a recorder, tapes, and the writings available for guests! What could be more modern!

On January 27 I arrived at the Honolulu Airport two hours ahead of schedule because of strong tail winds. The airport was completely deserted at five o'clock in the morning. All the passengers who had expected to have friends meet them found no one there at all—all of them except me. There, waving to me in the dark of that early morning hour with two beautiful leis to greet me were Emma and Joel, and thus began those unforgettable and memorable days.

The three of us spent part of every day in meditation, or I sat alone with Joel, meditating, while he dictated answers to his mail. Sometimes there would be a full hour's lesson, and it was then that he said to me, "This time you are going to get the works. When you leave here, you will be graduated and you will heal as you have never healed before."

Every morning I left the hotel in time to pick up Joel's mail at Pawaa Station in Honolulu and arrived in Kailua by group taxi shortly after ten o'clock. Emma always came over, and we would have lunch, talk, some relaxation, and then more work.

It seemed to me that I should exhibit a reasonable degree of good manners and not outstay my welcome so, many times during the day, I would say, "I think I should be leaving."

Joel's response was always quick: "Why should you leave? No, no, stay."

After this had happened several successive days, I finally told Joel that I wouldn't suggest leaving again, but that he would have to tell me when to go. Usually Joel, Emma, and I went out for dinner, and I would return to my hotel about nine or ten o'clock at night. To have almost ten hours a day of study with Joel for seven weeks was an unbelievable privilege. I could never have dreamed that on my seven subsequent trips to Hawaii I would be blessed with months of such close work with my teacher, an opportunity that was of the greatest significance in my own spiritual unfoldment.

It was just two days prior to my arrival that the unfoldment on mind, which later was incorporated in *The Thunder of Silence,* came to Joel:

Mind forms its own conditions of matter, body, and form. Mind imbued with truth is the law of resurrection, renewal, regeneration, and restoration.

He hammered away on that idea hour after hour, and one day at 22 Kailua in the midst of it, he sharply asked me, "What truth?" The incisiveness of his tone left me speechless, and I found no words to reply, but again he said, "What truth?"

Finally out came a very limp, "The truth that there is only one power."

At this point Emma interjected, "Why Joel, you are scaring her half to death."

"Well, it's far better that I scare her now than that some dread disease come along later and frighten her."

During February of 1957 *The Kailua Advanced Class* met in Joel's home on Monday, Wednesday, and Friday mornings at ten o'clock, with about seventeen students attending, most of whom lived on the Islands. Of this experience I wrote to my sister, "Joel has never made the healing work so clear as in this class. It is something that every earnest student should study very seriously. He is going deeper and deeper into the mystical life, and always his one concern is with the principles. Nothing else matters to him. I knew he was a great teacher, but how great only these weeks have revealed. I pinch myself sometimes to see if it's really true that this is happening to me. Every new unfoldment is explained first to Emma and me, and then we hear it again in the class. Joel goes over and over it for us."

These eventful weeks were made even more exciting when on February 8, 1957, Joel talked to Floyd and me about marrying Emma. Undoubtedly, there must have been an understanding between them for a long time, but he had never spoken of that possibility to me before, although I had long expected it. That afternoon, however, he said that he was going to ask her to marry him, which he did that very night.

A great attachment had sprung up between them during the years that Emma had worked with Joel. Those of us who were close to him were happy because we felt that having a loving companion would bring comfort and joy to this man who gave of himself so freely to the world. Emma's radiant countenance the next day confirmed that he had carried out his resolve and that she, too, was happy.

A day or so later, when he talked with me about getting married, his comment was, "I've never made anyone who has closely touched my life happy, and I don't want to make Emma unhappy, too."

I am sure that The Infinite Way world must have thought that the woman who married Joel would have a life of bliss, but I knew even then that it would not be too easy for Emma because Joel was very positive in his ideas and in some ways a very demanding person. He was adamant about having things done the way he thought they should be done—but so was Emma, and she had worked with him long enough to know his ways.

A few days later they took me on a drive around the entire island of Oahu and during that trip Joel told me that he had worked out an arrangement in regard to what should be done if anything happened to both Emma and him at the same time and he also explained my responsibility in carrying out his wishes. One of them was that I should continue to prepare a monthly *Letter* as long as students wanted it, but under no circumstances was I to be a lady bountiful and distribute such a *Letter* gratis. Students would indicate how much they wanted it by their willingness to pay for it.

It was obvious that the little house at 22 Kailua was too small for Joel, Emma, and her son Sammy, so before they were married Joel and Emma went house hunting. They found a charming two-level house on Halekou Place in Kaneohe. It was in very bad condition and needed a great deal of work done on it, but it had thirty feet of picture windows overlooking the mountains, a superb and breathtaking view that was ever-changing. In addition to the large living room, the house contained a kitchen in need of modernizing, three bedrooms, one of which Joel used as a study, and one bath on the main floor, and on the lower level a room as large as the living room, a bedroom, and a bath. The large room on the lower floor adequately took care of the hundred students who came from around the world to attend *The First and Second Halekou Classes* held in August.

Emma and Joel were married by a friend of Joel's, Rabbi Segal, in the rabbi's home on Joel's birthday, March 10, 1957. Emma looked beautiful as always in a blue taffeta afternoon gown she had purchased the preceding October in Chicago and had worn at the 1956 class there. Just six of us were present at the short and simple ceremony at which Floyd and I were the witnesses.

In the course of the conversation at the buffet after the ceremony Rabbi Segal spoke to me about the classes Joel was to give that August at Halekou Place and said, "I suppose you'll be back here for those classes."

Astounded at the idea that anyone would think that I could afford a second trip to Hawaii in one year, I replied, "Oh, no, I don't think so. I've been here." At that time I thought of a trip to Hawaii as a once-in-a-lifetime experience.

Across the room Joel heard me and called over to us, "She thinks it takes money," implying that it took consciousness and not money. This I learned, because with very little in the form of material resources, in that one eventful year I made three trips to Hawaii.

Late in the afternoon Emma and Joel went to the Royal Hawaiian Hotel to spend a few days there and invited me to go along with them for a visit. At least six different times in the next couple of hours I said to them, "Well, I think I ought to be leaving."

But each time Joel said, "Oh, no, don't go."

Finally on the seventh time I said, "This is your wedding day, so I think I ought to go."

His response was, "Well, after all we are not a couple of kids, you know, so stay."

So stay I did for several hours and went back to my hotel only to change and get ready for the wedding dinner at the Royal Hawaiian that evening.

In his diary, which he gave me in October, 1960, Joel made the following entries about his marriage and honeymoon:

> March 10, 1957, Emma and I were married by Rabbi Alex-
> ander Segal in his home in Honolulu, Hawaii. Present were

Rabbi Segal and Mrs. Segal, Mr. and Mrs. Floyd Nowell, Miss Lorraine Sinkler, Sammy Lindsay (Emma's son).

March 15, 1957, we flew to San Francisco, visited with Emma's daughter and her husband, Geri and Lt. Cdr. Jack McDonald, and Emma's son Bill Rustin and his wife Dorothy. Then flew to Tulsa, Oklahoma, to visit the Olney Flynns, then to Chicago for a visit with Lorraine Sinkler, New York with Walter Starcke, and then flew to Europe.

London for lecture and classwork and Chichester with the Henry Thomas Hamblins; Manchester with Roland and Gertrude Spencer, and lectures. Edinburgh, Scotland (with the Masters) and lectures. London with the Walter Eastmans, Mary Anthony, Earl of Gosford, classes again.

Then still flying, Switzerland; Rome, Italy; Munich, Germany with Marianne Lange and the children.

Back to London to receive honorary membership in the Lodge of the Living Stones (Leeds).

To New York, May 31, San Francisco, and home in Hawaii June 8.

Joel had found his traveling companion. He said that life without love is empty, just as life without freedom is empty. To be an individual walking up and down the earth not loved and not loving is not life: it is a living death. Love makes life worthwhile.

6

Journeys in Time and Space
—and Beyond

To those on the Path, and Joel was on the Path long before
he came into the world as Joel Goldsmith, there are no
accidents. Nothing takes place by chance; everything is according to divine order. The divine Consciousness, in-
dividualized as every person, knows what is necessary each
step of the way. Every experience, which a person who
carries on a great work has, serves to provide the requisite
equipment so that he may fulfill his unique function in the
divine Plan.

So Joel's time spent as a salesman cannot be discounted
or looked upon as lost years. As a salesman he was a good
one, he knew he had a good product, he felt he had only
to show it to a customer to have it accepted, and he always
presented it with an overflowing exuberance that was conta-
gious.

This same attitude carried over into his work in the
spiritual ministry. He never resorted to high-powered advertising of any kind, knowing that the worth of his product
would carry it to recognition, and his product was the fruitage of his conscious union with God. That needed no fanfare and none of the gimmicks so frequently used to capture
the fleeting attention of the public. He was building on a

firmer foundation than that, for his was a movement in consciousness.

Yet like the master salesman he was, he never lost an opportunity to present his product to those who had eyes to see and ears to hear because he never felt that it was he who was presenting it. It was always this Thing within that was living Its life as him, doing the work. He trusted implicitly in It and because of that trust was guided by a wisdom rarely found.

Joel's early career as a salesman, traveling the United States and Europe, was no accident but a preparation for subsequent years of traveling the world carrying The Infinite Way message. Perhaps, too, all this traveling was an outer evidence of a journey within that reached a destination only to find the next one beckoning him on.

On his journeys he drank in the wonders of nature: majestic mountains that dominated the horizon, fruitful valleys, flowing rivers, the glory of the heavens, and vastness of the oceans. Then, too, there were the man-made creations: imposing architecture found in temples, churches, and mosques, and city buildings old and new. To all these his response was, "After you have seen them, then what?"

The inanimate objects of nature and those man had made could not hear his message, and for him the message was the all-important thing, so it was never the works of man that held his interest, never nature except insofar as he saw in it an example of a principle. People were what counted. To him a world without people was but an empty shell. Fifty-five years of travel served only to reinforce this attitude.

While he recognized the futility of much of the traveling that was done by people for the purpose of sightseeing and education, separate and apart from people, most of it was of such an ephemeral nature that usually no lasting impression remained. Only when a person begins to discover people does he discover a reason not only for traveling but a reason for living.

To Joel, everyone on the face of the globe had something of a unique and individual nature. There is not a person anywhere who has not something within his being of value to someone else: something to give or something to share. He found it fascinating to come into contact with students all over the world and also to discover how great was the bond with many who were not yet students, how men and women everywhere were seeking much the same goals, how they all wanted the same things out of life, and how nearly all of them experienced frustration and unhappiness until they found something worthwhile, and that something worthwhile was always what they found within themselves and in one another.

If we are to find God, if we are ever to discover the kingdom of God, we must find it where it is . . . within you and me. This is what makes life worthwhile: the discovery of God in man. Many have searched for the Holy Grail, for God, but nowhere in the history of literature or religion has anyone ever discovered God except as he has discovered Him in man.[1]

Students flocked to his classes wherever he went, whether he remained at home in Hawaii or traveled to the far corners of the earth. He could have been kept busy day and night, month after month, with those who came to him in Hawaii for instruction, but his mission was to carry this work to all who were receptive and responsive wherever they might be. Many persons could not at a given time pull up stakes, leave their families, or have sufficient time or financial resources to go where he was, so he put on his winged heels and went where they were. This he did primarily for those whose goal was to be reunited consciously with their Source, who sought that lifting of consciousness which contact with a spiritual teacher could give. His travels averaged from 35,000 to 65,000 miles a year: thirteen times to Europe in twelve years and three times around the world, not counting the numerous trips abroad during his business career.

Some of these trips seemed at first to be only foolhardy adventures, to have neither rhyme nor reason. But Joel was living by Grace, and that Grace expressed Itself as inner instruction all along the way. One such example was in 1953 when seated at his desk in Honolulu he heard the Voice within him say, "Go to New York in November. Wait there a few days in December, and then go on to London."

To be instructed to go to New York was understandable because there were a few students there studying the writings who had expressed the hope that he would someday give a class there. But what about London? There was no reason for him to go to London, none in the world. As far as he knew, there might be twenty, thirty, or forty persons in all of England who had found The Infinite Way writings, but beyond that he had no knowledge of any work there or of any activity. Despite the inner persistent question, why London, he went right out to the airline office and ordered a ticket for New York and London.

In New York that November there were four classes, two morning classes especially for practitioners and two evening classes which brought to a focus the principle of the Middle Way—not this and not that. When the classes ended on November 30, he had nothing to do but sit around, wait, and look at the Christmas decorations on the streets, not really knowing what his next step should be, although he had ordered his passport and it had been delivered to him.

On the fourth of December a message from within, which he interpreted as the Voice, came again and said, "Go tomorrow." So he went to the airline office, picked up his ticket, and the next day was on his way to London. There he went directly to his hotel where a suite had been reserved for him and sat down to talk to God: "Father, I'm in London. I have nothing to do here, no one to see, no mission, but here I am. Now why? What do You want me to do in London?"

As he sat there waiting, all of a sudden that same Voice said to him, "You know a dozen people here who are reading *The Infinite Way*. Why not send cards to them and let them know you are here? They might like to talk to you. They can call you on the telephone or visit you."

"Now, that's a good idea. I'll do that. I'll go downstairs and get some postcards."

The next thing he heard the Voice say was, "You have a chum over in Germany you haven't seen in many years. Why don't you let him know you are here and that you are going to visit him before you go home?"

"Good, I am going to do that, too," and he did.

Then again, "You've been wanting to meet Henry Thomas Hamblin. Why not write him a letter?" Through that letter an appointment for Thursday was made to visit the venerable Mr. Hamblin at his home about two hours from London.

That Thursday morning he awakened early and was ready to go out to see Mr. Hamblin, but before he left, the mail came and with it a letter from Sweden, forwarded to him from Hawaii, informing him that there were twelve students in Stockholm who were reading *The Infinite Way* and some of them would like a little help. They casually mentioned that they had received *The Infinite Way* from a Christian Science practitioner in London and asked him if he would ever think of coming to Sweden to talk to them. This coincided with what Mr. Hamblin later told Joel about the practitioner in London who was buying fifty copies of *The Infinite Way* at a time and sending them out to friends and patients.

After Joel returned from seeing Mr. Hamblin, he made a call on this practitioner, who was very happy to have a visit with him. The important question in her mind was how she could get the other Infinite Way writings because, inasmuch as she was living in England, the problem of exchange seemed almost an insuperable barrier. Joel offered to send her all the books she needed as gifts, but she did not want them that way. That violated the sturdy independent character of her British background. She wanted to be able to pay for them, so she suggested that he arrange to have the writings published in London, asking him to talk to Mr. Nagle of L. N. Fowler, Ltd. to see what could be done about it. As a result L. N. Fowler began publishing Infinite Way writings, which made them easily available to students in the United Kingdom and the Commonwealth. All this new activity had come out of a Voice saying, "Go to London." Humanly it did not make sense, but spiritually it was divinely ordained, a rich experience outwardly while all the time the inner work was going on.

January 7, 1954, Washington Hotel, London:
The miracle of overcoming time and space, the great me-

chanical and atomic progress of this age, these are but the outer experiences of an *inner* growth in consciousness; and the wars, panics, sins—these are the breaking up of the material dream as Spirit continues to express Itself, Its nature and character. We then must *welcome* these outer inharmonies as evidences of spiritual growth and this holds good in individual experience.

January 19, 1954, 9:50 A.M.:
The Voice bade me meditate. It announced Its presence as He that would now and henceforth be with me as teacher, protector, support, before me, beside me, and within.

Lifted me to higher consciousness. . . . Work is to be given me as necessary.

The same physical experiences came as with previous teachings and ordinations. The same "evidences" of the Presence.[2]

Nineteen hundred fifty-four took Joel to Portland, Seattle, Chicago, New York, England, and Sweden for lectures and classwork. He was beginning to feel the grandeur of the message that after only eight years was encircling the globe and finding receptivity and responsiveness everywhere. It was in London that he met Walter Eastman who has since spearheaded the work in England and coordinated it throughout the British Commonwealth. After the completion of the work in Stockholm came a visit with his long-time friend Hans Lange in Munich, Germany, and then on to Zurich, Switzerland. There arrangements were made for the publication of *The Infinite Way* in German. The important work of this journey completed, he decided to visit Rome, where he had not been since he had become interested in spiritual work, then Athens and Istanbul.

In Damascus there was an unforgettable experience as he walked the street called Strait. It was a crowded evening. There was not room to walk without being jostled on both sides, back and forth, and yet despite the crush of the crowd, the spirit of Paul descended upon him, and it was he who was walking right beside him. Joel was not really walking on a street called Strait: he was in the consciousness of Paul. Those days at Damascus were like living in the actual consciousness of the early Christian era.

From there he went on to India, Hong Kong, and Japan, flying from Japan home to Honolulu in eleven hours, an amazingly short time back in 1954.

On this first journey around the world, he made notes about some of his experiences:

November 15, 1954, 6:50 P.M. Stockholm, Sweden:

Tonight will be the final Infinite Way talk of a series of lectures and classes which started March 3, 1954, in Honolulu, Hawaii. . . .

What the future holds I do not know. . . . I have no fixed schedule of travel, and at this moment no "feel" of what is to come. It is as if a curtain were lowered over November 21, and I could not see beyond that date, nor do I know the meaning of this strange situation.

Have not been able to give any forwarding addresses for mail beyond Munich. I am certain it portends something of an important nature, and two suggestions continue to intrude upon me, either one of which is possible. It may mean the end of my earthly experience. This suggestion has seemed a possibility for several weeks. From the physical standpoint, my health is seemingly perfect, but this may mean nothing.

The second suggestion seems more probable: that this talk tonight ends the message of The Infinite Way as we now know it, and November 21 may open its newer and higher phase. It is for this that I have been waiting and praying since 1950.

Since that year, I have known that there is another step beyond which The Infinite Way will find its Christhood. Never for a moment have I been satisfied or content with the revelation since 1950. Always the conviction, and *sometimes* the inner promise, has been present that I would be given the next and final demonstration. Actually I know now and have occasionally felt this Ultimate, but not yet realized It.

So, at this moment, I wish to make my complete surrender to God. As I have heretofore dedicated myself to the search, the practice, the unfoldment of Truth or God as revealed in the message of The Infinite Way; as I have let myself be the instrument for this work up to the limit of my understanding; so now I surrender myself—life, mind, soul, and body—to God in full. Whether on earth or beyond, whether in the body or out, I surrender and wait, and promise obedience and faithfulness, as God gives me the capacity, since of my own there is no strength, no power, no character, no will.

I surrender this physical sense of life to be ordained here or hereafter in the service of God.

I surrender every vestige of self that Self may be revealed on earth as God's will directs, maintains, and sustains Itself as my life, mind, soul, body, and being.

To this end, O God, take me and mine and *be* me and mine as Thou wilt. Let there no longer be me and mine except as Thou art me and mine.

Take me unto Thyself that Joel may be dissolved and Thy selfhood, the Christ of Thy being, be known on earth or beyond. Be Thou me.

November 15, 1954, later at 11:30 P.M.:

Well, the final evening is completed. Now I look forward to whatever vision unfolds or whatever activity of the Spirit reveals Itself. Amen.

November 26, 1954, 3:00 A.M. Baur-au-Lac Hotel, Zurich, Switzerland:

Finally, after complete desolation since November 16, after the last talk in Stockholm, It came, lifting me above the sense of flesh, out of every discord, Christed. A release from the small "i," a release from personal selfhood and its cares and ills. Christed—there is no other word to use.

The color and appearance of my face changed; the body took sharper form, a new aliveness. Until 4:30 A.M., I was in the

Spirit. Then I slept until 9:00 A.M., and even now I am not the
same man as lived yesterday. I have been reborn. Thank You,
all the Power that is, thank You. My heart yearns to express
gratitude in an adequate way, but there is no way. Thank You.
Peace, peace, to the world of flesh, His peace.

November 29, 1954, 3:30 P.M., in flight to Rome, Athens, Istanbul:
The degree of realized or attained consciousness is the degree of God-government experienced.

December 2, 1954, 3:00 A.M., Beirut, Lebanon:
Attaining spiritual consciousness, one is freed of all desire
for person, thing, or condition, freed of all desire for effect.
One's consciousness then is entirely on Cause, appearing as
effect spontaneously without will, thought, or desire.

December 13, 1954, Calcutta, 10:30 P.M.:
Live as a master, and the power will be given to *be* a master.[3]

The following year was a relatively quiet one with most of the time
spent in Hawaii until the latter part of the year. From all over the
world invitations were coming to Joel to give lectures and classes,
but it was his custom never to respond to any call until he was given
the go-ahead signal from within. One morning, while he was giving
classes in Kailua for a group of local and visiting students, the decision was made to go to Detroit, and he immediately called for a
reservation. The next day, however, he was told definitely that he
was not to go to Detroit, but to Chicago and Seattle, and to that was
added Portland. Those were the orders—Chicago, Seattle, Portland
—but again he did not know why. Nevertheless he ordered tickets
to those cities in that order. Further instructions came that the work
that April was to include not more than twenty students in Portland,
ten to twelve in Chicago, and twenty in Seattle.
When the work was over in Chicago, Joel said to himself, "Now
why did I have to go all the way to Chicago to make those six or

seven hours of recordings that could just as well have been made in Hawaii?" Then he realized that it had to be in Chicago and Seattle because in those cities were the students who could bring forth the particular message that came through him in those four sessions of *The 1955 Chicago Private Class* and in subsequent sessions of *The 1955 Seattle Private Class.*

In August, 1955, Joel again found himself on his way to London with brief stops in Chicago and in New York where arrangements were made with Harper & Brothers to publish *Living The Infinite Way* and where a few informal talks were given at Frances Steloff's Gotham Book Mart. Then came several weeks in London, a few days in Holland, and on to Sweden. From Europe there was a hop down to South Africa where he spent several weeks before completing his second journey around the world.

Another trip around the world came in 1956, only this time a new place was added: Australia. Although he thought he would be meeting between thirty and forty students of The Infinite Way in all of Australia, instead he found more than this number in Perth alone, a city that he had not even known about. He had been invited to go there and had accepted the invitation because he thought it was near Melbourne and Sydney where he was already scheduled to give lectures and classes. It was—just a mere 3,000 miles away. So he made a 6,000-mile trip there and back just to keep his promise, but he felt that it was worth it. The Spirit had gone before the message and made Its way for it. This was Joel's last long trip as a lone traveler. After his marriage to Emma, she was his constant companion on these journeys.

The news of Joel's divorce and remarriage met with varied reactions among the students. Some thought this an unwise move, fearing that it would destroy the close association with their teacher which they treasured. Others looked upon it as a protection to Joel and were happy that he had found a loving helpmate. As students became acquainted with Emma, opinion was again divided: some found her beautiful, loving, and possessed of deep spiritual consciousness; others thought of her as cold, unapproachable, and interested primarily in the material things of life. They felt that Emma acted as a barrier to shut them out and keep them from having ready contact with Joel. This I never felt. In fact, I myself would have found it difficult to have someone around me as much as I was around them. When I told Emma and Joel that I felt as if I belonged to them, Emma's warm, reassuring response was, "You don't know how much you belong." And Joel added, "Well, I guess Lorraine is getting to see just about everything, and some things no visitor ever gets to see: 22 Kailua Road. No money can buy entrance there."

Joel's first overseas trip, not too long a one, with Emma, his new traveling companion, was their honeymoon in 1957. But in 1958 a very extensive program of classes had been set up, including Australia, which was to be Emma's first trip there. The preceding November Joel and Emma had invited me to come to Halekou Place early in December, spend Christmas with them, and then stay on to be in the house with Sammy while they went to Australia. Sammy was only thirteen and, knowing that he would be well taken care of, Emma could leave with a light heart for this extended trip.

Of his experiences on this trip "down under" Joel wrote:

> *January 17, 1958:* Pan American Air to NSW, Australia, with stops at Canton Island, Nandi, Fiji Islands.

Arrived 7:30 A.M. in Sydney and was met at airfield by Joyce Burns Glen and at hotel by Mary Samuel. Had a tail wind of 100 miles an hour and was an hour early, but flight pilot gave us an hour over the harbor, suburbs, and city. The groups of Infinite Way students gave us two round trip air tickets on turbo-jet PAA from Sydney to Melbourne, Adelaide, and Perth and back to Sydney and thirty pounds cash for "pocket money."

> *January 19, 1958, Sunday at 11:00 A.M.:*

Joyce and Mary drove us out to the beaches, Jonah's at Whale Beach for lunch. Returned at 3:00 P.M. in 94 degree heat. At 4:30 a hurricane wind of 93 miles an hour struck with thunder and rain for only fifteen minutes, but did heavy damage at the beaches. Temperature dropped fifteen degrees in fifteen minutes. January 20, cool and clear. In room until noon with reading, meditation, and preparation for first lecture this evening. For two days (since Bible reading in plane) have been working with the principle revealed in the story of Sapphira: "Thou hast not lied unto man, but unto God." Here is the spiritual weapon against deceit, aggression, etc.

January 20, 1958, Monday evening:
Talked to 65 students. Theme: why these fears of the world? Is the creature (form or effect) greater than the Creator, the Infinite Invisible?

January 21, 1958, Tuesday evening:
A tremendous follow-up to last night. In the middle of the night awakened with the significance of "the atheism of material power" and "saw" the deadness of materiality in the presence of the Word. "They forsook God and burned incense before false gods"; and they worshiped and feared the power of material force and thereby forsook God.[4] Again 65 students, about 25 of them not the same as the first night.

January 23, 1958:
Left Wednesday evening, January 22, for Melbourne, Victoria. Mrs. Samuel and Miss Ellen Samuel met us at the airport in Melbourne and drove us to the hotel. They came down at noon on January 23, and we lunched at the hotel and spent the afternoon driving through the parks, suburbs, etc. Had tea, and back to hotel. Evening dinner just the two of us and a quiet evening alone.

January 26, 1958, Sunday:
A day of reading, meditating, struggling. Then 8:00 P.M. class and fine message: serving God instead of expecting God to serve man. . . .[5]

Early morning, realization of the nature of the transcendental Presence which has been with me since late 1928, and which has led, fed, taught, and guided me all these years.

February 5, 1958:
Adelaide class especially good, especially on treatment and spiritual healing principles.

February 6, 1958:
Flew Viscount (T.A.A.) to Perth, Western Australia. Met by Mr. Webb and students.

February 7, 1958:
On the plane to Perth, began a spiritual experience. Unfoldment from within impossible to put into words, but acting as freedom from material sense or a deepening of spiritual consciousness. Probably a release from corporeal sense would describe it.

February 8, 1958:
In meditation a vision came of *physical* sense (as if an entity) knocking at the door of consciousness for admittance. Also the capacity to reject the entrance of physical sense. It seems as if all discord is wrapped up in the term *physical sense.*
Start program in Perth with lectures at 3:00 and 8:00 P.M. today at Seekers Centre.

February 9, 1958, Sunday, Perth, Western Australia:
Impersonal Christ healing. Every person or condition appearing to me is personal or physical sense, knocking at the door of my consciousness to be accepted *as* person or condition. *Consciously* reject every appearance. Understand that this is neither person nor condition, but physical or personal sense seeking admission as real existence and seeking to *personalize* itself. *Never let error personalize itself* or you have no principle to demonstrate. Never admit personal or physical sense into con-

sciousness *as* person, name, or condition. Immediately recognize personal sense *as* impersonal error trying to personalize itself by having you accept the appearance as person, race, nation, or condition.

This rejection of the appearance or recognition of the appearance as personal sense prevents sympathy, pity, or fear. This is the secret of impersonal Christ healing.

February 10, 1958, Monday:
I see as God sees, His own perfect being expressed as man and the universe. I see the One appearing infinitely as individual being. Finite or corporeal sense seeks to present itself as finite, corporeal person, thing, or condition. But, I say, Rise, show Thyself as Thou art. I say, Rise—walk. I say, Thou art whole. Corporeal sense presents pictures of limitation but understood as corporeal sense without form this limitation disappears.

We start Closed Class. Have had lecture audiences of 200, and 60 in Closed Class. Albert's Book Shop and the Methodist Book Depot report fine increasing sales of our books.

Will leave Thursday, February 13, 11:30 P.M. for Sydney, then New Zealand. Wonderful day in Sydney. Plane delayed so took Joyce, 'her father, and another student, and Emma to see Dame Sybil Thorndike in a play. Ellen Samuel of Melbourne, just married since class to Peter Temple, came out to have coffee with us at airport 1:30 to 2:30 A.M. Then we took off for New Zealand. . . .

Left Monday A.M. for Hamilton, but could not land due to flooded airfield (three days of rain), and came up to Auckland. Have two talks here at Higher Thought Temple. Fly Friday to Fiji Islands for holiday.[6]

The holiday was not too happy. The heat was excessive and made even more unbearable by the very high humidity. Joel and Emma occupied a villa on the premises of one of the largest hotels there, but the villa proved to be a glorified name for a grass shack without air conditioning and with six-to eight-inch-long lizards running back and forth around the ceiling. To keep tolerably cool Emma wrapped herself in wet towels. After such an experience Hawaii looked like the paradise it is advertised to be, and they were more than happy to return to Halekou Place.

After they arrived home from their six weeks in Australia, they asked me to stay on with them until it was time for me to fly back to Chicago to make preparations for Joel's three weeks of lectures and classes to be held at the Pick-Congress Hotel. From Chicago the three of us went on to New York for work there, after which Joel and Emma flew to England and the Continent.

While they were in Holland, where Joel had been invited to give a talk on August 29, 1958, for the International Healing Conference at Zeist, sponsored by the Queen of the Netherlands, he meditated with Mrs. Hoffman, the spiritual healer and teacher who had achieved considerable notoriety because of her reported influence upon the Queen.

After that meditation Mrs. Hoffman told Joel, "Go home, Joel, and remain quiet. Stop work until after November. Your work, heretofore confined to certain groups, will now take on a wider sphere of activity. Do not let the people draw on you or sap you. Keep more aloof. Wait patiently for November." This was a message that had already come to Emma.

Joel immediately obeyed, and on September 1 Emma and Joel left Holland by air, stopping in London for dinner with the Earl of Gosford and leaving at midnight by polar route for San Francisco. A week later on September 7 they were home in Hawaii where he lived very quietly during the remainder of 1958, canceling all the classwork scheduled for the rest of that year, although on occasion he did teach small groups in Hawaii.

Those seven months in Hawaii, waiting for the birthing of a new aspect of his work, were difficult ones for Joel, but it was a period of great inner unfoldment, as is evidenced by the following notations:

September 14, 1958, 7:30 A.M.:

The Inner Plane

Close your eyes and realize that here within yourself, you are complete Being, Self-sustained, Self-maintained. From here within your Self come the issues of life. Here within me I have meat the world knows not of; from here within come teaching, direction, wisdom, support, supply, guidance, and what ye shall eat and drink and wherewithal ye shall be clothed. Nothing shall by any means fail as you seek only within for your all.

Here within you, *I* am established as your life and being. This is your immortality! *I* am your immortality. Here is your authority: *I* am your authority.

Release yourself now, completely, to *Me*. Release yourself from thought and *I* will speak. This is the full surrender of the self.

September 14, 1958, Sunday, 12:30 P.M.:

Effects of The Infinite Way

The Infinite Way message and activity are embodied in the writings and the recordings which constitute The Infinite Way. The effects of this Infinite Way are first felt in the consciousness of those who read, study, and finally practice this way.

The consciousness of the individual will at first rejoice in the new Light which dawns within, and many minor discords dissolve and disappear from experience. Then, later, as meditation becomes deeper, and human sense is stirred and roused, there may come a period of inner conflicts, and latent sins and diseases are brought to the surface, erroneous traits of character are self-revealed, clarification begins, and finally peace reigns, both in mind and body. It is at this point that one's friends, relatives, and business associates begin to feel the healing influence of The Infinite Way consciousness and to take on the peace and joy of this higher consciousness.

Now The Infinite Way student has found that he is taken over by the Infinite Invisible, that a Presence and a Power is governing, guiding, and directing. There is less and less dependence on person and thing of the outer realm, and a greater resting in the completeness and perfection flowing from within.

As one's life is more and more lived by the Invisible, consciousness expands, and The Infinite Way covers a wider sphere of influence and many near and far begin to feel and be spiritually healed and prospered by the consciousness of those who are now living under the wings of the Almighty.

Eventually all the world will be governed "not by might, nor by power," but by the divine influence of The Infinite Way.

For all the centuries of humanhood, man and his universe have been swayed by two powers: good and evil. Now, under the spiritual government of The Infinite Way, the manifestations of the sons of God will commence, and these will no longer be powers—neither evil powers nor good powers—but the reign of Grace will appear on earth.

There may be, and probably will be, an infinite number of religious teachings, teachers, and churches, but all shall gather together to acknowledge one Spirit, one God, and the divine rule of His grace. Some will worship with hats on and some with bare heads; some will wear shoes into church while others will enter barefoot or in slippered feet. Some will carry the crucifix, some the star of David, and others one of an infinite number of symbols, representing some concept of Truth. But all will unite in humble spirit to acknowledge that man shall no longer live by bread alone or by the sword but by the grace of God without taking thought, without supplication, but in the understanding that He that is within you already knoweth your need, and it is His good pleasure to give you the Kingdom.

In this higher consciousness, there will be no need to seek God's power, for nowhere in heaven, on earth, or in hell will there be the sign of any other power for there will be none.

Indeed, even now, there is no power but God, no power in evil or disease except as man's ignorance of God's allness has caused him to accept the ancient temptation to believe in two powers. God's grace dispels this ignorance and thereby lets mortal man "die daily" and be reborn here and now as the son of God, returned unto his Father's house, robed again, and wearing the princely ring of divine sonship.

September 30, 1958, 2:00 P.M.:
Alone in the house. Have dictated mail for several hours, meditated.

And then I experienced myself as life independent of form. In that moment, I realized how unimportant it is what my form of the moment is: male or female, white or black, Occidental or Oriental, human or animal—as long as I am and as long as I can sit at the feet of spiritual existence. To worship God or love God supremely, to know the spiritual nature of the universe, this is to sit at the feet of the Master, this is to live—the form is of no consequence.

November 16, 1958, Sunday at Halekou:
From the time of my first spiritual experience late in 1928, I have been given specific tasks to be accomplished, some on the Inner Plane and others outwardly.

First of those outer works was the healing ministry. During the sixteen years, 1930–1946, I stayed consistently with healing through spiritual consciousness, sometimes teaching the way to others ready for that experience. During these years other works were given me to do on the Inner Plane, and this past week I have seen the completion of the major work given me. Each of the others has previously been completed but the major work was twenty years in coming to full fruition.

The Infinite Way was given me as an inner revelation to be brought to outer fruition, and the part of this mission concerning its outer expression is now completed. All of the writings are either in publication or have been accepted for publication.

Foreign translations proceeding slowly but surely. The Tape Work, something entirely new in the teaching, is established. All of the work given me to do thus far has been completed. Its establishment (The Infinite Way) in human consciousness is now a matter of unfoldment. The Inner Plane work is also completed, and my release has been given me.

In the nearly thirty years of this work, one point should be made clear for all to understand: all the work given me to do both on the Inner and outer planes has been performed, completed, or accomplished by Whatever gave me the work. It truly has gone before me at every step. It has given me the necessary wisdom, direction, support, and supply. I have been only Its instrument, an instrument *through* which or *as* which It could perform Its mission on earth.

If, in any way, I have suffered pain or problems, it has been in the degree that personal selfhood had not been completely dissolved. Those closely associated with me who have been made unhappy will understand why I cannot censure them or criticize. It must have been difficult being around a man living in two worlds and unable to make himself adjust to one world.

November 24, 1958, Monday 9:00 A.M.:
Have remained here quietly, and today received the realization of *I.*

December 10, 1958, Halekou:
During the past week had one day of tremendous illumination but without a specific message beyond the Presence. Today comes a sense of the imminence of a new dimension of Consciousness. This new dimension has been promised me, first in 1952, then postponed to 1953, then to 1955. Ever since, it has been knocking at the door of consciousness, but not quite broken through. Now it is promised for now and the immediate future. It carries with it a new work on international levels and a contact with another Source different from any heretofore experienced. Today there is a dropping away of the

old way, the old work, the old responsibility. It is a sloughing
off experience.[7]

Finally in April, 1959, after waiting an endless seven months, a
clear-cut message was given him:

April 8, 1959:
A new day dawns today for The Infinite Way. *My* consciousness becomes the consciousness of The Infinite Way, of its
activities, of its personnel. *My* consciousness is now the activity
of The Infinite Way, of its workers, of those who work in its
vineyard. *My* consciousness influences and activates The Infinite Way in every part of the globe.[8]

May 9, 1959:
Relying on the help of students and receiving "a common
sense" reply threw me into a whole new vision. There is no
need to look for help from the students. To inaugurate the
reign of Christ, do not enlist the aid of men, not even to
believe in the need for students to heal or teach or serve. The
reign of Christ is all that matters. No need for disciples, or
apostles, or helpers. *Let Christ reign.*

June 4, 1959, Halekou:
Take up the error of nature mysticism and its explanation.
Take up the nature of the visible universe (Genesis II) and
mind control of it. Take up "yoke" and its relationship to our
work.
The importance of treatment (correctly understood) is the
development of spiritual consciousness.
Today: we are building our body now, the body of ten years
hence, and the body of "after here." Also business activity,
profession, etc.
The yoke of Christ carries the burden of the practitioner.
Infinite Way treatment does not project thought from practitioner to patient. Treatment is within one's self (projection is
mental).

June 8, 1959, Halekou:

An activity under God's grace results in *perfect* fulfillment because it is God's will being done with you or me as God's instrument. God gives us His wisdom, guidance, support, and all that is necessary. The main point is: do not undertake a day, a move, an activity, until the meditation has resulted in *conscious* awareness that you are acting under Grace.[9]

With these instructions, beginning with *The Hawaiian Village Closed Class* in July, Joel spent the rest of 1959 traveling across the United States and on to England, giving the specific healing principles of The Infinite Way which are unique and basic to its teaching. Over and over he emphasized the principles of impersonalization, the nothingization of the carnal mind, neither good nor evil in form or effect, and the nature of spiritual power which brings with it the realization of the nonpower of all effect.

August 4, 1959, London, England:

Throughout the world today individuals and groups are seeking what they term a spiritual power with which or through which to bring peace on earth. Others are engaged in seeking and developing mental powers with which to control others, individually and collectively, for their personal gain, power, or success. Individuals in organized movements are at present advertising publicly that they have discovered this mental power which controls people and things and that they willl teach it to anyone, in one case for the price of a $3.50 book and another case for $2.00 per month.

Needless to say, those who really know the secret of mind-power (if they are men of integrity) will not sell such knowledge for any price, and if they lack integrity they will demand what is beyond the means of most men.

One organization which beyond all dispute knows the secret of mental control of individuals will impart it only to a limited, select group of men whom they develop and train and keep under their own control. This is easy because once an individual learns the power of mental control, he himself becomes a master of the ignorant and a slave to those who he knows have this knowledge. It is like the possessor of the nuclear bomb who becomes master of those who do not have it and a slave living in fear of those others who have it.

In every age there have been individuals in groups which knew, taught, and used mental powers, both those who used those powers for good and those who used them for selfish and sometimes for evil purposes. Always these men and groups of men came to an end.

This is brought about in three ways: (1) mental inertia inevitably stops many from continuing the practice; (2) the reaction upon those who use mental powers for selfish or evil purposes finally wrecks the mental and physical health of the user of these powers; (3) ultimately there come into existence those who know the ultimate truth or secret of life, and this renders the mental powers useless.

It is clear now that regardless of how widespread the knowledge and use of mental powers has been in our age, it has not resulted in universal peace or prosperity although it has given a temporary dominion and prosperity to such individuals and groups.

Those who now are seeking a spiritual power which they hope they can use for world peace will fail in this age as they have in all previous ages. The secret of spiritual power is not to be found in the way that it has been taught and is being taught.

The secret has been revealed five times in recorded history. It may be that some others have discovered the secret, but it has not been recorded. Because of its very nature, it can only be taught to those who have been adequately prepared for the revelation, and therefore, four discoverers of the secret of spiritual power have been able to teach only a few students, and those could teach still fewer, so that each time the secret has been lost in the third generation after its discovery, and with too few at any one time to accomplish a universal peace and prosperity.

The fifth recorded discovery of the secret of spiritual power and its application to human affairs has taken place in this present century and is being demonstrated and proved on a scale beyond anything known before this era. Again, because of its nature, the world as such cannot accept it or believe it; therefore, once again it is being taught only to those who have accepted a long period of preparation for the revelation and a further and longer period for practice.

There is evidence now that what the world would call miracles are being brought about by these students. Just as a magician's tricks are not miracles to the performer, so these miracles are not miracles to those who know the law.

When Steinmetz predicted that the greatest advance in the twentieth century would come in spiritual knowledge, he knew that this secret was again to be revealed and he knew that the age-old problems of human life were nearing solution.

The secret of life is being revealed to the world, veiled for its protection. Wherever there are those who have eyes to see, the veil is lifted, and another is started on the path of realization and demonstration of truth, and another link is formed in the chain of spiritual illumination. Miracles of grace are about to be revealed.[10]

After the specific work in 1959, teaching the principles, Joel felt that the metaphysics of The Infinite Way had been so thoroughly and completely presented that there could be no question in any student's mind as to what the basic principles were, and that left him free to take the students deeper into the mystical realm of conscious union with God. That is why the classes from 1960 to 1964 were all devoted to leading the students out of the metaphysical into the pure mysticism of The Infinite Way which had been revealed to him in his first great initiation.

It was the giving of classes that necessitated traveling to far places, in itself an arduous task. To make that aspect of it less difficult, Joel and Emma always traveled as comfortably as possible, going first-class and availing themselves of the best accommodations in the best hotels in whatever cities they stayed. He was working fourteen hours a day and needed his human comforts cared for so that the body was well out of mind and all his energy could be devoted to the work.

Wherever they went, they were met by students, and the suite they occupied overflowed with flowers, candy, and fruit, offerings of love laid at the feet of their spiritual guide. His days were filled with appointments and the ever-present mail. No matter where he went his mail reached him, usually fifty to a hundred letters a day which he scrupulously answered. These letters were for the most part from persons seeking healing, an aspect of his ministry which he considered of the utmost significance and therefore he never failed to answer every such call for help. He was an enigma to the mail clerks in the hotels because he received so much mail. One of them had the temerity to inquire why there was so much mail for him, and Joel's answer was typical, "Oh, they just want to borrow money from me." This was like Joel because he never wore his ministry on his sleeve.

When the mail came in, his custom was to open every piece of it himself, reading it as it was opened, and putting each letter aside until all the mail had been read. Then began the laborious task of answering these letters. When he traveled, his mail was done by hand, but at home in Hawaii it was dictated for the most part on a Stenorette machine and given to a secretary who typed it in her home and returned it promptly the next morning.

Knowing that those who wrote to him were waiting for an answer, he always replied immediately. Each time he opened a letter and read it, he paused to realize whatever was necessary in the particular situation being presented to him. When he wrote or dictated the answer to the letter, he went through the same process, and when he read over his answer, there was a third period of realization for that person.

With all of his intensive program and the traveling hither and yon, Joel remained, on the whole, amazingly well physically, but occasionally some problem arose. Whatever its nature, however, it did not stop his work. One evening in London he had to go on the platform wiping his nose with a handkerchief.

All right, let us confess right now. I have not ascended, but is it not wonderful to know that we have found a principle whereby we are virtually not in bondage to anything, and if we are for a few moments, it does not last? If for one reason or another some of these minor things bother, let us not deny them. Let us be grateful that we have something with which to meet them.[11]

When Joel and Emma went to Australia and New Zealand in the latter part of 1960, there were the usual delegations of students to meet them, but when Joel got off the plane he had no voice whatsoever. This had happened just fifteen minutes before the plane was ready to disembark, and here he was in Australia with many students he had never met before, all eagerly waiting for their spiritual teacher, and all he could do was to point to Emma. He had the same experience in New Zealand.

In a situation like this, his innate honesty was evident. He could very well have had Emma say, "Joel is not speaking today. This is his day of silence." That would have labeled him a great spiritual light. But all such subterfuge he recognized as foolish nonsense entirely beneath the integrity and dignity of a spiritual teacher.

I had a claim, and it hit me that way, and there is no wonder when you keep talking ten and twelve hours a day, seven days a week. Vocal cords have to give out some time, and this time they did. But that night I was on the platform, and the voice operated perfectly. Then when I got off the platform, it would not work. That went on for several days, and I suppose they thought, "Well, this is a fine how-do-you-do."[12]

On November 7, 1960, he wrote me from Adelaide, Australia:

I am having a heavy struggle here with what appears outwardly as a summer cold (it is summer here—beautiful summer weather) but I can hardly sit up or hold up my head. Really tough. Inwardly it is no doubt frustration or grief.

Many great truths are being revealed to me, but without easing the burden. How I long to tell what is coming to me!

As a matter of fact this continued until they returned home to Hawaii, and from there Joel telephoned me in Chicago, asking me to give them some help, and on December 7, 1960, sent the following telegram:

Both experienced complete healing. Love and gratitude.

In a letter of the same day, he wrote:

Dear Lorraine:

Thank you for wonderful work.

With me it went this way: until 9:00 A.M. next morning, no evident change. Then, while dictating, a flare-up of the throat —and in five minutes a clean, perfect healing, without the smell of smoke left.

Emma awakened in the morning free of pain—and has remained so.

Beautiful work, Lorraine—just beautiful.

On the trip I had no difficulty except voice and throat, and that was so severe at times, I thought we would have to cancel several times and come home. Always managed to squeak by —but without healing. Now that the throat is clear, am fresh as a daisy, and could start all over again.

But not Emma. The last month was a terrible strain on her. As you know, when the temperature goes below 70, she needs fur underwear—and when it goes over 80, she suffers. And this trip was all above 80 or under 70—and she went from cold to cold to cold, one after another. She is clearing up now after a week at home, but she is tired.

Geri, Sue, and Sam are living at 22 Kailua Road, so we have

the home alone. All quiet and clean as a new pin. So Emma should get something of a rest this month. Bought a used station wagon, or whatever you call them, for the kids. Meanwhile I dictate 60 letters a day to keep McQuay busy. She is also typing all the classwork of Australia and New Zealand and will send you two copies each. Once the desk is cleared, will have very little to do.

Nothing exciting is taking place, in fact, seems like a dull routine—for there has been nothing of interest in the mail, just routine stuff. With *Thunder* [*of Silence*] on the press, excitement has ended. Do not know how long I could stand this uneventful existence.

My office looks nice. Have taken Sam's room for my office. New desk and chairs and white carpet on the floor and new window drapes. Very nice—all of it.

From March 29 to May 1, *every day* is filled with lectures and classwork and special groups. Will probably extend California work to May 15. This will give the new Harper book a break, and *Conscious Union* and *The 1959 Letters.*

Well, I do not know the opposite of Walter Mitty—but I am he! Just a quiet, peaceful, unthinking, lazy guy—going no place in particular—and not in a hurry to get there, Mr. Routine himself in a dull sort of way.

Our united love to you and Valborg,

Joel

In March, 1961, Emma and Joel left Hawaii to go to California for classes and for what they expected would be a two-month trip away from home. Instead of that, the trip was prolonged far beyond that time because something was operating in Joel's consciousness that would not permit him to go home. In fact, he took advantage of every kind of excuse not to return and found reasons for going here, there, and the other place. The here, there, and other places included the Northwest—Seattle, Portland, and Vancouver—Tulsa, Oklahoma City, Chicago, Washington, D.C., and finally New York.

Then I ran out of excuses, and there was no reason not to go back home. So I had to say to Emma, "Well, don't you think it would be nice to visit London for a week or two as long as we are this close? We are only a puddle-jump away."

So we jumped the puddle. Inwardly I was being nudged or plagued by something that wouldn't come out, something that wouldn't come to the surface, and I couldn't go home and be quiet because it didn't seem to me that it would come that way, so it was necessary to keep traveling.

Friday night it came. You have it all. Certainly when I went on the platform, I little dreamed that anything like that would come forth, and even now I can't believe that it came out, but it did, and that is what I had been waiting for, for nine months. It's what I'd been trying to get born, and the reason I know it so surely is that I have had my peace ever since.[13]

The lesson that just wouldn't come out but finally did became known as *The 1961 London Closed Class,* Reel II, Side 2, and was later incorporated into the book *A Parenthesis in Eternity* in the chapter called "Living Above the Pairs of Opposites." The day after this important message was given, Joel received the manuscript of the August, 1961, monthly *Letter.* He wrote to me in amazement, asking me where it had come from because he said that that was the very message he had delivered the night before. Several years later when Joel read that chapter in the manuscript of *A Parenthesis in Eternity,* he wrote that it did something for him.

Most people would believe that such a trip as Joel and Emma took in 1961 would be rather an aimless kind of idle time and vacation, but wherever he went, places were provided for him for lectures and classwork, and there were opportunities to meet with smaller groups of long-time students. It was during that trip that he watched the opening of Infinite Way work in Munich, Berlin, and Frankfort, and arranged for some of the writings to be published in Germany.

Usually plans for Joel's trips were made far in advance. All hotel reservations, reservations for lecture halls and classrooms, and even airplane reservations were made and paid for months ahead of time. The only thing that was not determined was the specific hour of departure, because plane schedules change from time to time. But the day and the date were settled a year before, and nothing interfered with a single one of those dates. Every trip was made on schedule, never having to wait over an extra day, never having to postpone any work, never being delayed.

Joel was a very wise man and, in spite of living in a dimension that few people ever touch, he was down to earth and completely practical when it came to dealing with the affairs of this world.

"Take no thought" has nothing to do with the orderly planning of your life. That really must be done, and you must know in advance when to arrange for your holiday or if you are going to make a trip to a class somewhere or something of that nature. But even though you are making those arrangements, always hold yourself in readiness for a cancellation without concern because you must be trusting the fact that there is an invisible Presence that knows far more than you do and can govern and guide. . . .

Tomorrow afternoon at five o'clock we are to be on a plane bound for Hawaii, and you know we are taking thought about that today because we have to go to the airplane company and fill out forms. We have to be sure that everything is packed and in order and that all the details of this work are closed. There is a lot of taking thought about that. . . .

But where the "take no thought" comes in is to take no anxious thought. Do not be concerned; do not be fearful; do not be worried. Plan what you are doing, but always with the realization that there is Something greater than you working through you. Even though you are taking thought and making your plans and arrangements, be perfectly willing that they be changed.

In other words, regardless of how right a move may seem

to you that makes you plan ahead, even to buying tickets, do
not ever be disturbed if at the last moment something comes
up to change those plans completely because it will merely
mean that there is some reason behind it, some reason which
could not have been known a month ago or a year ago or
whenever the planning was done.[14]

With television available, most persons would never have made
the effort to travel from one end of the world to the other as Joel
did. But if he had gone on television he felt that he would not have
had the kind of an audience he had when he talked to relatively small
groups eager for the message.

Do you think the world would listen? Or would it mock?
And you know the answer. So when I travel the world, and it
takes me years and years to go around this world to give the
message out to small groups, remember I could be doing it in
one night in a studio in one city and never have to leave home
and save all this trouble and travel and all this work. But it
would be of no avail.

And so I go only where there are those who are showing
their dedication to the message through their study, through
their practice, and through their financial support in some
way. Everyone with whom I talk has shown me that he
has an interest in truth, an interest in this message, and
that he is giving of his time and of his efforts and of his substance.

Then, to those, I can say this and be sure that they understand it and that they receive it and that they respond to it, and
that they will put it into practice and "tell no man."[15]

Whatever would fulfill the work was what Joel did, and always this
Thing within him dictated what that was. I remember that as I was
about to go forth on my second speaking tour, dubious as to what
I could add to the message Joel had given in such completeness, he
said, "You go to bring consciousness." And this was the basis of all

his traveling: to carry consciousness, the consciousness of Omnipresence, Omnipotence, and Omniscience to those who could not come to him. To fan the Flame burning within each and every one into awareness was his purpose.

Yes, Alec is quite right that there are groups working for us, not only on the outer plane, but on the inner, since I am sure you know that the entire message of The Infinite Way has been given from the Inner Plane and has been promoted around the world from the Inner Plane, and I have just been the messenger boy whose expenses they pay to travel. Probably they could have used some other traveling man as well, but it just so happens that I love to travel so much that they probably wanted to reward me for some good deed that I did unconsciously at some time or other.[16]

Joel could have had his following multiplied and the fleeting adulation of crowds if that had been what he was seeking. Instead, he chose to have the few, but the few who would be able to carry on in his absence. He felt that if he could develop as many as twelve good teachers and practitioners while he traveled the earth, they would be worth more than half a million followers. He would not have felt this way if popularity or money had been the guiding factor.

Surely, you can get richer off a half million followers, and if wealth or popularity means anything, I guess that is it. But if personal accomplishment means something, which it should, to a teacher, then believe me if he could turn out two, three, four, five, or six who have really and truly caught the spiritual and mystical vision and can work with it and can go out, first of all, to heal others and then to teach others, you have done a far better job, even though the rest of the world will not know about it.[17]

It took love; it took dedication; it took devotion. It took an unselfedness to carry this message to so many places, to be willing to leave a comfortable and beautiful home, the gentle climate of Hawaii, and the easygoing pace of the tropics. But while Joel liked comfort, that was not preeminent in his mind. Comfort did not matter to Joel. It was only the work that mattered, and all else was subordinated to it. Always he was the gallant traveler.

7

A Movement in Consciousness

The principles of The Infinite Way came out of an experience, and to Joel this experience is The Infinite Way. Principles intellectually taught and imbibed lack the vitality and vigor of living truth. Only as truth flows from the innermost recesses of an individual's soul out into awareness can it have the life-giving qualities of truth. All else is but the dead letter.

The principles he could present, but they would never reach beyond the level of the mind unless they were given by a teacher who himself was alive with the Spirit and was imparting them out of realized consciousness. Then the student who is prepared and has attained a state of readiness will be able to take those principles into consciousness and there receive from within the seal of authority.

Joel Goldsmith had the unique ability, reserved only for those who themselves have had the deepest experiences, of giving the world the most profound truths in the simplest of terms. In fact, the principles of The Infinite Way can be summed up in three little words: one, as, and is.

Oneness is a cardinal principle of The Infinite Way, a oneness which is so basic and all-inclusive that it cannot be sidestepped with any ands, ifs, or buts. There cannot be that one all-inclusive Being and some other power, presence, cause, law, substance, or activity.This simple principle of One is so infinite and expansive that it includes life from every aspect. Because God is the all-power, there are no other powers. Because God is the all-presence, there is no other presence. Because God is all-wisdom, that Wisdom need not be enlightened and is instantly available.

Secondly, but equally important, is the word "as": God appears *as* individual being and *as* the spiritual universe and all that is included in it. There is nothing outside of or beyond that One, that One which is infinite, unlimited, pure Consciousness. That One appears *as* the many, but always the essence and quality of the One are the essence and the quality of the many.

The final word is, "is." God *is;* Grace *is;* harmony *is;* perfection *is.* How much good is shoved away by believing that good *has been* or *may become* a part of a person's experience at some future time or state! But all the Reality that exists, exists now. There will never be more of God than there is now, never more of good, wholeness, abundance, perfection, infinity than at this moment. Living in this moment of *isness,* the next moment unfolds as a continuity of Grace.

Since the Experience had come to Joel through meditation, it is understandable that in The Infinite Way meditation should become the basic technique for attaining awareness. Through meditation, a student who is sufficiently dedicated and one-pointed can touch the center of Being which for lifetimes has been buried under the debris of that human consciousness which is constantly swinging between the pairs of opposites: good and evil. New insights into facets of the all-embracing One are continually being revealed in meditation, and these lead a student to go deeper and deeper within to the very center of Life.

Rightly called infinite, this teaching is a mystical way leading to that illumination which brings conscious oneness with the Source. Its ultimate goal is perhaps best revealed in that statement found in the front of all Infinite Way writings and also in this book on page 61.

No individual or group of individuals in The Infinite Way is ever bound by the chains of membership or obligation to any person or any organization. "Illumination dissolves all material ties and binds men together with the golden chains of spiritual understanding." There is no ritual or creed, nothing to which one need adhere. Each person's developed spiritual integrity is his authority and rule for action.

To Joel, the message of The Infinite Way was universal, and he looked forward to the day when its principles would be universally adopted. From long experience he was certain that this could never be possible if this teaching were encased within a church organization, because then it would lose its vitality and universality. The Infinite Way could be universal only as its principles were available to each and every person, to each and every organization of every nature without restraint or restriction. Inasmuch as there is no Infinite Way organization, there is no possibility of setting up a barrier or a protective attitude on the part of any group or church. Its purpose has never been to destroy organization of any kind, but only to be the leaven that would leaven the whole.

Joel realized that when he was gone there might be persons of good will or ill will who would seek to crystallize these principles into the form of an organization. Knowing the dangers inherent in that, he prayed long and hard over it. In fact, someone once wrote him, "I have a wonderful idea for an unorganized organization." It was just such do-gooders that caused him deep concern until the Voice spoke, "Be not concerned. The Source of this work will never permit it to be organized, and whoever tries to do that will be removed."

The possibility of someone's attempting to organize The Infinite Way was often in Joel's mind, as can be noted from the following letter he wrote me after the 1964 class in San Francisco while aboard one of the ships of the Matson Line bound for Hawaii, March 13, 1964:

Am sure you saw the significance of what is taking place in the message. It is still necessary to be alert or the students will entangle themselves in organization while congratulating themselves that they are free. Then they will blame me for their stupidity. Trying to keep the message organization-free is as difficult as keeping the Hebrews of old from a king. "The natural man" wants a golden calf, a crucifix, a flag, or a king.

At times considerable inducements were made to him to organize The Infinite Way.

I have been offered $10,000 several times, $75,000 once, $200,000 twice, and refused. What shall I do with it? If I give it to our workers in the cities and towns, they lose the import of the message: God is your *consciousness*—draw on it. We need no subsidized success.

Shall I perpetuate The Infinite Way? Why? Individual consciousness—understanding it—contacting it—realizing it—this is The Infinite Way.

And personally I neither need nor desire such sums. While this cannot be told except to our "inner circle"—on this last trip I proved "no purse or scrip." Went all around the world, 38,000 miles, without using my American Express checks. Each country supported its own activity, including my expenses. And left enough over in England and South Africa to start the next trip.

If I had a religious corporation to accept tax free gifts, we would soon have a large fund and more responsibilities![1]

To a student who sought Joel's advice about ensuring what she considered the proper succession to leadership of The Infinite Way Study Center she had established in Washington, D.C., he wrote:

Dear Friend:

I am under divine orders to the extent that there shall be *no Infinite Way organization,* and for seventeen years of Infinite Way activity I have had to be very, very alert because so many attempts have been made to organize in ways that students did not realize would *lead* to organization.

At this time I wish to bring this to your attention. If you have a Study Center or a Tape Group, and if you have furniture or furnishings, or Infinite Way tapes and books, please *make a will* and leave these to your estate and not to any successor. You can stipulate in your will that your executor can offer any of these things for sale to anyone who wishes to buy them and, if you like, you can even designate a very low price in order to make others able to buy them and continue the work if they wish, but in this way you will be ensuring that there is no succession, therefore no organization, therefore no legal entity.

To have an Infinite Way Study Center is the demonstration and the activity of the consciousness of an individual, and no one can inherit this from you. And no one can succeed to a Tape Group you have established, because this is also the externalization of what you have established in your consciousness. But if you have a stock of tapes or books available, whoever it is who wishes to purchase them and undertake the activity makes it an individual activity of his own.

In kingdoms there is a succession, and it is for this reason that there are no kingdoms left on earth. Even in England it is really only a form, and the reason is this: no son and no daughter of a king or queen can inherit their parents' consciousness. It is for this reason that no provision is made for a president to hand down his office to a son, and so it is in business. How many fathers have tried to hand down their businesses to their children, and how few have succeeded! And in spiritual matters this is even more true.

As the leader of an Infinite Way Center or an Infinite Way Tape Group, please understand that you cannot confer your demonstration upon anyone else. Therefore, you will never train anyone to succeed you.

Aloha,

Joel[2]

Joel knew that The Infinite Way would survive only because of the degree of attained consciousness of those who practice its principles. He needed a hard core of a few students with a healing consciousness who could carry on the work and show its truth by the fruitage.

Many years before when my one goal had been to find God and when I disclaimed any interest in the healing aspect of this message, Joel told me that healing is the proof of the truth of it. Later I learned how right he was and what an important part the practice of the principles of spiritual healing plays in the development of spiritual consciousness.

Joel rejoiced when anyone appeared on the horizon who was willing to undertake the responsibility of the healing ministry. Even greater was his joy when a student with a healing consciousness was willing to go forth carrying this message to the world. Despite this, however, he would never give financial aid to anyone who stepped out into the world with the message, because he knew only too well that each one must go forth on his own consciousness and be maintained by that consciousness. The work would be doomed to failure if those who carried it on did not have the developed consciousness necessary to show forth fruitage, and continued in it only because they were getting support from some kind of headquarters. When a student had a healing consciousness, he knew that that student would have no further financial problems and would be able to maintain himself.

No provision was made by Joel for authorizing practitioners. The healing consciousness itself would be the only authority, and therefore, a student would stand or fall on his own consciousness. Going through one class or a dozen classes was no assurance that the healing consciousness had come into full bloom, and until it had, any kind of authorization or diploma would be of no value.

Joel was adamant in regard to any kind of proselyting. He never used advertising or ballyhoo of any kind to bring this teaching to human consciousness. His was the way of prayer and meditation. He trusted that the prayer which has within it no condemnation, which opens consciousness, and which invites the world to find spiritual peace would be sufficient to spread the work of The Infinite Way. Students were cautioned against trying to carry The Infinite Way to the world. They were warned to go only where they were invited and never to invite themselves to any city, community, church, or center in order to introduce the work. If they were invited and advance information assured them that there would be a sincere understanding and welcome, then they were encouraged to go and share whatever it was they had, but they were urged to be sure to go to bless, to increase, to share their light rather than to try to recruit followers by taking them from an established group to swell their own ranks.

While there is no organization in The Infinite Way, nevertheless there is a small staff made up of a secretary, Geri McDonald, who is Emma's daughter; Bessie Anderson, who since 1958 has made the tape recordings and kept the books; and the editor. That comprises the entire staff, surely a small enough one. But there is no organization; there are no memberships; there are no rules; and there are no regulations. Joel's innate passion for freedom evidenced itself in this work which was closest to his heart.

There are fifty or sixty thousand families studying The Infinite Way, and humanly I could say, "If each one of you will give me five dollars a year for a membership, then I could avoid the market place and just say, 'I live in the spiritual atmosphere.' " But if I asked them for five dollars a year, more or less, I would have forsaken my spiritual atmosphere. I would have come right down then to the market place, and doubly so because I would have been putting my reliance on man, on his good will, and on numbers instead of on this divine Grace.[3]

The Infinite Way has always met its financial needs without any fund-raising drives and has been amply provided for by the Consciousness that brought it forth. Consciousness has always been the secret of The Infinite Way and the basis of its operation, and that realized consciousness has taken care of every need.

The grass-roots of The Infinite Way are found in the tape groups which have sprung up throughout the world. Anyone who wishes to do so may begin a tape recording group. These tape recording groups nearly always meet in homes, but in large metropolitan areas, occasionally the tape group leader rents space in a hotel or office building to make the meetings more accessible to students. Those who come listen to recordings of Joel's classes and lectures, have meditation before and after the recording, and gather together freely with no obligation except that of love. There is no discussion, no music, and no advertising. All a person interested in starting such an activity has to do is to sit quietly and wait for those to come who want to participate.

Beyond that, there are the groups scattered around the world who engage in daily prayer activity for the opening of consciousness to spiritual realization. These usually are persons who have been students of The Infinite Way for a sufficiently long period to have gone beyond a primary concern for their own welfare and are now willing and ready to take upon themselves specific work for the world: to regenerate human consciousness and to bring about the second coming of the Christ as the consciousness of individual being universally experienced. These groups also have no organization, no authority over anyone else, and the composition of a group in any one place may fluctuate from time to time.

To this day The Infinite Way has remained an unorganized activity, a movement in consciousness. Joel felt very strongly that he would far rather see students make mistakes than to set up rules and regulations to guide them. In this way each person would maintain his individual freedom, and if he did make mistakes, he could learn from them and go forward, but there would be nothing binding him and holding him to a state of consciousness which he had outgrown or not attained.

If a student is a member of an organization, he unconsciously or even consciously relies on his association with the group or he may rely on someone who has gone further along the Path than he, and in that way he has found himself a new Messiah. This inevitably creates a sense of separation from God. The whole of The Infinite Way is dedicated to turning man within to discover that the Source of all that is already exists within his consciousness, and he needs nothing outside, nothing external to that consciousness.

8

☙ Out of Consciousness into Form

As The Infinite Way became more widely accepted, there was an ever-increasing demand for Joel to give lectures and classes. At first the classwork was confined to California, and it was out of the classwork in San Francisco and Los Angeles that five of his most powerful books came: *The World Is New,* originally *The San Francisco Lectures; Conscious Union with God,* formerly *Metaphysical Notes; Consciousness Unfolding; God the Substance of All Form;* and *The Master Speaks.*

Joel's early writings began with letters, some of the earliest to his first tuberculosis patient—trunks full of them—and thereafter his letter-writing continued all his life.Many of these letters to patients were written in longhand. In fact, he wrote so many letters that he once said to me, "Here's one signature that will never be a collector's item. There are too many of them scattered around the world."

Many patients and students wanted to have a message from Joel at regular intervals, so he began sending out a weekly mimeographed letter, highlighting principles of spiritual living and healing. It is not surprising, therefore, that from the inception of The Infinite Way, a monthly letter to students should evolve as part of the work.

In the early days of The Infinite Way a former minister

was drawn to the work in Los Angeles. His considerable knowledge of the Bible appealed to Joel, and with his support and encouragement, the minister began the publication of a monthly letter called *The Infinite Way Messenger,* to which Joel contributed an article regularly. In 1953, when the relationship between them had become very thin, Joel severed it completely. Toward the end of that year he wrote a letter to all those who were subscribing to *The Infinite Way Messenger,* announcing that it would be replaced by a monthly letter written entirely by him to be sent to students who expressed an interest in receiving it.

Joel was now living most of the time in Hawaii and considered that his home. There he gave talks to little groups of students, and these talks, which were recorded as *The 1953 New Hawaiian Series,* were transcribed from the tapes by Ruth Maberry, who edited and assembled them into the English edition of the book *Living The Infinite Way.* She also prepared and edited the first Infinite Way monthly *Letters,* those of 1954, 1955, and 1956.

One of the gems of all the writings is a little pamphlet called *Love and Gratitude.* While Joel was walking toward the Alano Hotel in Honolulu to give a lecture, it was as if he heard a voice say, "Won't you buy me a flower, just a little flower?" He turned around to see who wanted this flower, but there was no one there. Again he heard it, but this time it was coming from some place within him. His face lighted up and he said, "Sure, sure, I will." He turned around and ran back a block to Auntie Bella's little flower stand and asked, "Please, may I have a couple of little carnations?"

"A couple of little carnations? Sure!" She took two, put a wire around them, and Joel walked down the street with these flowers in his hand, all smiles, realizing that he must have looked very foolish to the rest of the world. Up he went on to the lecture platform, put the little flowers there along with his Bible, and began a talk which lasted for more than an hour. Later he was told that he had been talking about love. A whole hour talking about love!

When it was over, he could not remember one word of it. Everybody just sat there. Joel waited and waited, but still nobody wanted to move, so finally he made the break and walked to the door. Even then the students were reluctant to leave their seats, because they had heard a message that to them was electrifying. Nobody seemed able to tell what had been said except that it was about love. One couple, who knew him well, told him that that was the first time they had ever heard him mention the word. Unfortunately, the tape recorder was out of order, and not a word was caught.

Some time later in Seattle, in a class, he found himself again talking about love, and for the second time the tape recorder was out of order and the lecture was not recorded. This time, too, nobody could tell him what he had said. The next Sunday morning he was certain that he was going to talk about love, and he did. The operator of the tape recorder, however, became so interested in listening to what Joel had to say that she forgot to turn on the recorder, and still not one of them could remember what he had said. The following Thursday night the recorder was in working order and the message which comprises the pamphlet *Love and Gratitude* came forth.

These talks on love were Joel's first conscious knowledge of what love is, and the reason he did not know about this before is because he thought love had something to do with persons, and he found out that that was not true, that all love is of God.

> You may not believe me when I tell you that I debated as to whether I should put a price of fifty dollars a copy on *Love and Gratitude* or fifty cents. I had the feeling that that booklet had in it that which in time was going to thunder down the ages, and I know now that that is true. There is something in that booklet that will change the lives of those who catch the point, and it will change their lives drastically, dramatically, and quickly.
>
> The thought that came to me was: who would believe that for fifty cents? For fifty dollars they will say, "I wonder what is in it that I am supposed to see," and they would study more carefully.
>
> But a moment or two later the thought came: that is human reasoning. If it is truth, turn it loose for nothing, without money and without price, and if it can be published for fifty

cents without loss, publish it for fifty cents, and those who have eyes to see and ears to hear will find it.[1]

Another priceless little gem is *The Deep Silence of My Peace*. This, too, came out of a class-experience in Seattle. Extras were on the street that night, not with one banner headline but with three, indicating bad news in Korea, a threatened railroad strike, and the possibility of a nation-wide telephone strike.

When Joel went on the platform, the air was thick with apprehension and concern. Everyone in the room was coughing and moving and there was every kind of restlessness, which is not usual in Infinite Way classwork because so much meditation precedes every meeting that the students are usually at peace when the class begins. But there was no peace that night until Joel began talking, and out of the peace generated by that talk came such a silence that he called this pamphlet *The Deep Silence of My Peace*.

Ever since my first meeting with Joel in 1949 there had been the close relationship of teacher and disciple which never ended, but in 1955 to that was added a new relationship, that of author and editor.

Well do I remember that morning in April, 1955, when Joel arrived to give a private class at the Chicago Infinite Way Study Center, a class for which I had been given strict instructions to invite only ten persons. After he was comfortably settled in at the Palmer House, he handed me the transcription of the tape recorded lecture, "The Easter of Our Lives," and asked, "Will you and your sister Valborg work on this and get it ready for a little pamphlet?" There had been no previous indication of anything such as this, so we were taken completely by surprise, but readily agreed to do the job.

Interestingly enough, the preceding Christmas following a deep spiritual experience, it had come to me that I should "leave my nets," give up my career as a teacher and public school administrator to devote my life to The Infinite Way. It was a decision that I of myself did not make: that Something within pushed me into it. I waited several months to let this inner guidance crystallize, finished out the school year, and then on July 4, 1955, turned in my resignation, leaving a position in a school system where I had served successfully, happily, and joyfully for twenty-five years. The class Joel gave in Chicago that April served to reinforce a decision that proved to be the turning point in my life.

At the close of the class Joel asked me to drive him up to Michigan to visit Joseph Sadony. Those two days of driving back and forth gave us long hours together in which to talk about the work and also gave me the joy of listening to him reminisce hour after hour about his early experiences, his new home in Hawaii, and much about Emma, who by that time had come to occupy an important place in his life.

On the trip to see Joseph, Joel talked about an idea he had for another book on the Bible, similar to *Spiritual Interpretation of Scripture,* and asked if Valborg and I would edit it. Whenever he asked me to do anything with the manuscripts, my sister was always included because at one time he said, "You and Valborg are so much one that you are really one person with two heads and four hands." A couple of years later he wrote to her, expressing his deep appreciation for her work:

December 14, 1957

Dear Valborg:

We are so happy to have Lorraine here with us. . . .

Am so thankful for all your work on The Infinite Way message. Am sure you realize that what you are doing is for eternity. With two books coming through Harper's, the world gives greater recognition to the message—which otherwise would have had to "seep" through over a longer period of time. . . .

To have had a hand in these writings is to be established in eternity. No man can take this glory from you. Happy holidays.

Joel

Although I was still teaching at that time, I worked late into the night, accumulating material from the tape recordings of Joel's classes that I had purchased, and Valborg and I worked on that material every spare moment we had. From any number of tape recordings we put together bits here and bits there of enough material to form what we felt would be an excellent first chapter for such a work, but it was never destined to serve that purpose. The following August, on his way to New York to see his publisher, Harper & Brothers, Joel stopped off in Chicago to give me the opportunity of meditation with him and further instruction. He graciously accepted an invitation to speak at the Study Center, which my sister and I had opened a year before. As he was about to begin speaking, Valborg reminded him that this was the first anniversary of the first Infinite Way Study Center in all the world, so he launched forth into an inspiring and illuminating talk on the subject of study centers and spiritual unfoldment.[2] He was in Chicago for three days, and I spent most of the waking hours talking with him and working with him.

Before he left for New York, he handed me the transcriptions of that momentous *1955 Chicago Private Class* held earlier in the year and also a transcription of the seventeenth tape of *The 1955 Kailua Study Series,* saying, "I am supposed to have a book ready for L. N. Fowler of London before I leave there in October. This is all I have. Can you and Valborg do something about it?" And of course we agreed to do it.

Then a little later on in the conversation he brought out a few scattered papers that had no rhyme or reason to them and said, "I am also supposed to have a book for Harper & Brothers on the subject of meditation. This should have been ready before now, but you can see that there is really nothing here that can be used. Can you do something about it?"

Again my answer was, "Certainly, we'll be happy to." And so in that three-day visit the responsibility for the preparation of two books was turned over to us with no instructions beyond having something for Joel to give to Harper & Brothers on meditation and something for L. N. Fowler.

Since the most pressing job was the book for L. N. Fowler, we decided to get to work first on that. But after Joel left for New York and before there was much opportunity for us to get started, he telephoned me from New York and asked if I would fly there to do

some work on *Living The Infinite Way* which Harper had expressed
an interest in publishing, but which they said needed two new chapters added to it. "I have ordered a first-class ticket for you on one
of the big new planes, and you will leave Chicago at four o'clock in
the afternoon and be in New York at seven. Take a taxi to the
hotel."

When he called it was then eleven o'clock in the morning, and it
would take well over an hour to drive to the airport. Furthermore,
it was necessary to make arrangements for someone to take over the
Study Center in Chicago while I was gone and to see that that person
had the keys. So it was a hurry-up rush job to get off and get on that
plane, my first flight. In fact, until April of that year when I had
driven Joel to the airport, I had never been inside an airport, let
alone on a plane.

In New York Joel said that he had decided to use the two chapters
we had prepared for the proposed new book on the Bible for *Living
The Infinite Way.* So right there in the hotel a typewriter was rented,
and in my feeble and inadequate typing I typed out those two
chapters for him to hand over to Harper. I spent several days in New
York working with Joel, talking often about the new book that we
were going to prepare for him on meditation.

John van Druten, who wrote the Introduction to *The Infinite Way,*
was a frequent caller on Joel. On one occasion when we were together in the hotel, I turned to John, for whom I had considerable
respect as a very successful playwright, and, because I was still at sea
as to what to include in a book on meditation, asked him, "John,
what would you include in such a book?"

The answer was not very satisfactory, and afterwards when I saw
Joel alone, he said to me, "Never do that again. Never ask anyone's
advice about what you are to do. Go within, and let the guidance
from within be your sole reliance."

When I returned home, both Valborg and I worked continuously
on the book for L. N. Fowler. Since I owned most of the tape
recordings of classes that had already been given and had heard
them many times, I was very familiar with Joel's work, but I had no
written transcripts of any of the tapes except *The 1955 Chicago Private*

Class and *The 1955 Kailua Study Group Series* Reel XVII. So I had to sit down, listen to the tapes, and transcribe such portions of these as would be suitable to include in the book.

Gradually as we worked on it, the pattern emerged. Certain principles began to take shape as specific chapters in the book, and in an amazingly short time it was ready for the final typing. Margaret Wacker Davis, a student in Chicago, offered to type half the manuscript for me. This was a great gift because my typing was of a very poor quality and not at all suitable for the preparation of a manuscript. I gave her the first part of the book, but it was not long before we discovered that her typewriter had different type from mine, and the two could not be used together. With that, she said, "Well, I'll just type all of it," a wonderful and ever-so-welcome gesture of love and friendship. From that time to this day, Margaret has typed most of the work sheets used in the work on a book and always the final draft of every book that has been published and also of every monthly *Letter.* Here was another example of Consciousness unfolding as whatever is necessary at the moment.

As soon as Margaret finished typing the manuscript, which later was entitled *Practicing the Presence,* it was sent to Joel in London. The following letters show how unstinting he was in praise of work he felt was well done.

> October 13, 1955
> Thursday 5:00 P.M.
> Washington Hotel
> London, W. 1

Dear Lorraine:

The manuscript just arrived, and it is far beyond my expectations. It is so good that I am giving it to the publishers as it is. That tells the story.

If I can, will write an Introduction as the book opens at heavy meat on the first page. If not, it goes as it is.

I do not know how you could do such a fine job in this short time except that God owns The Infinite Way and holds the hands of those who enter its consciousness.

There are no words of appreciation that are adequate; there is no gift that would say, "Thank you." I know that you and Valborg have really worked, and so to both of you I can only say that I know it also and am grateful. To both of you will come the blessing of spiritual fruitage.

Please accept the enclosed to give yourself a week-end holiday—with quiet, peace, and no work—and I mean it! . . . If writing more words could increase my gratitude, I'd keep on writing. Please read between the lines. This gives us a book to hold us over until *Meditation* is complete. . . .

For now—

My love to all

Joel

October 14, 1955

Dear Friend Valborg:

I will certainly not try to thank you in words for your devotion to the message or to the manuscript. Let me tell you my thanks in another way:

Back in the early 1930's—about '33 or '34—Nellie Steeves became my secretary *without pay*—typing ten copies of my weekly *Letter* and some of the letters to patients. She was still doing the mail and weekly *Letter* when it was 200 a week! And about ten letters a day of regular mail. Eventually she moved to California and did all my mail and the manuscripts of *The Letters* and *The Infinite Way* as a *real* secretary with portfolio! Then came Nadea to help with the start of The Infinite Way —and Minnie Law who did *Spiritual Interpretation of Scripture.* And then Emma Lindsay—and altogether about a dozen who are the real pioneers of The Infinite Way.

You are fortunate in that you will one day look back on these days with amazement, and we are fortunate that you are one of the pioneers of The Infinite Way, one of those who helped deliver the Child to the world.

Welcome—and heartfelt gratitude,

Joel

After that, work began in earnest on the book on meditation for Harper & Brothers which was finally given the title *The Art of Meditation.* I listened to every tape recording of classwork that I had, looking for material from the classes on the subject of meditation. Fortunately by this time, Jessie Porter of Vancouver, B.C., one of the first persons to invite Joel to speak outside of California, began sending me transcriptions of the tape recordings, typewritten copies which saved an immense amount of work. In addition to that, Bettie Burkhart began transcribing other tape recordings to relieve me of that chore, a work she continues to do.

Together with the hearing of the tapes and the taking down of what was suitable from them and these transcriptions of the tapes, work on *The Art of Meditation* proceeded. Bit by bit the three divisions of the book and the chapters necessary to be included in each subdivision unfolded as the material was assembled.

The first third of the book was ready for Joel to read at the time of the March, 1956, Steinway Hall Classes in New York. He gave this material to Eugene Exman, head of the Religious Books Department of Harper, who read it and liked it well enough to give the go-ahead signal for publication. Joel, himself, felt that it read beautifully, so beautifully in fact, that he said it covered up the TNT buried underneath. In a letter from Zurich, Switzerland, May 22, 1956, Joel wrote enthusiastically:

Dear Lorraine:

Your Part 2 is tremendous. Have written Exman that I doubt if the remaining chapters will influence the decision. But if he doesn't accept it, I will jump to New York in August and see other publishers who have expressed interest.

You have done a grand job. . . . There is certainly nothing I can see to change in the entire manuscript. Let us not have it so perfect it does not sound like Joel. . . . Heartfelt thanks and love to all,

Joel

And from Johannesburg, South Africa, he wrote June 14, 1956: "Have read 2/3 through, and it is magnificent. The further I go the better it gets, and it becomes the textbook I visioned on meditation and spiritual living—and not literature." Joel had a hang-up about his books becoming literature because he interpreted literature as something synonymous with dry and dull intellectuality.

By May the completed book had been sent to Joel, who was traveling around the world, and when a cable from him arrived with his O.K., the manuscript was immediately rushed to Harper. The book was released early in November, 1956. To celebrate its publication, Frances Steloff of The Gotham Book Mart in New York City had a coming-out party for it which Joel attended so that he could autograph copies and readers could meet him. This was like Frances, who for years had been introducing promising unknown writers to major publishing companies and thus helping to launch them on their careers. When Frances heard Joel lecture in New York in 1953, she was drawn to his work, and thus began a friendship, based on mutual understanding and trust, which lasted throughout the years. It was she who was instrumental in presenting Joel's writings to Harper & Brothers, a debt Joel never forgot. Frances Steloff has played a most significant role in The Infinite Way.

The following year, when Joel was reading *The Art of Meditation* to Emma on their honeymoon, he said, "God surely had Lorraine by the hand when she prepared this book for publication." His gratitude and appreciation were very real, as indicated in a letter to me from London, dated April 11, 1956, before *The Art of Meditation* was published: "Want a page in front as follows: 'Dedicated with gratitude to Lorraine Sinkler.' You have earned it. . . . And please tell Valborg I will write—I *am* grateful, even if it doesn't seem so."

This directive I ignored because I felt that it would not be appropriate. On November 22, 1962, however, Joel wrote me from Capetown:

Dear Lorraine:
    Today starts a large class with eight sessions and then home. . . .
    I have always desired that our publications carry a line to the effect that this book is edited by Lorraine Sinkler. Even new

printings of the old books should contain this. We will speak
of it again. . . .
Of course my recent difficulty was my own fault. I could not
rise above personalities and paid the penalty. Believe me—"as
ye sow"—is a *principle*. See you soon.

Love,

Joel

From that time on, beginning with *Man Was Not Born To Cry,* the
editor's name has been included in all new books published.

At the Steinway Hall Classes in 1956 when Joel had the proofs of
Practicing the Presence and when *The Art of Meditation* was well under
way, he told me that the classbooks—*First, Second,* and *Third San
Francisco Lectures, Metaphysical Notes, The Master Speaks, Consciousness
Unfolding,* and *God, the Substance of all Form*—would all have to be
edited and prepared for publication, one book every four months.
As he said later:

> While the mimeographed copies of the classbooks had all
> the truth that is in the classes, they were very poorly done, but
> that was as good as we could do at the time. There weren't any
> publishers in those days who believed that Infinite Way books
> were ever going to sell or that anyone would be interested in
> buying them, and therefore this was the only means we had of
> getting these notes in some form that the students could study.
> This work is spreading, however, and a book to be given out
> to the public now must be presented in a good-looking form
> and be editorially correct.[3]

As early as May, 1956, the editing of the monthly *Letter* was
beginning to loom on the horizon. Joel wrote on May 24, "It may
be necessary for you to take over the monthly *Letter.* . . . I would
be able to spend more time with you in Chicago and together we
could turn out good work. I could keep up with any amount of work,
but not with people, especially those students who can't work with
me."

In October the preparation of the monthly *Letter* was turned over to us beginning with the January, 1957, *Letter.* From that time on, the monthly *Letter* has been prepared in substantially the same way as the books: first, letting inner guidance determine what the subject of *The Letter* should be and then searching for transcriptions of Joel's tapes that would carry through on that subject. When *The Letter* was prepared in its final form ready for printing, it was sent to Joel for his approval and on to the place where a camera copy of it was made which was then sent to the printer. The monthly *Letter* is a most important part of Infinite Way activity.

> To me, our monthly *Letter* is a very sacred thing, very sacred. I don't think anybody knows how sacred except Emma and Lorraine because they have seen me with it as if it were a baby. The reason is this: it is not a piece of paper to be sent out to read. . . . That *Letter* is a sacred bond between me and my students. That is my way of having a correspondence course, only I can't believe in correspondence courses that are laid out and then every year sent out to the new students who come in.
>
> My correspondence course has to be written fresh every month, and then every year another correspondence course and then every year still another one. True, these *Letters* are perpetuated in book form because truth is in them, but I wouldn't be satisfied to say to you, "This is my correspondence course. I am teaching you with yesterday's manna." No, this is inspirational; this is instructive; this is to be practiced. And when I want to teach you spiritually, I want to do it spontaneously; I want to do it with something that comes through; I want to do it with something that is alive.[4]

Was it spontaneous? Yes, it was because while the material in *The Letter* might have been given a year or two or five before it found its way into print, when it was originally given, it was a spontaneous impartation to Joel from within. Actually, the only book that Joel sat down and wrote, and a great deal of that was taken from letters that he had sent out, is *The Infinite Way.* All the rest came out of class-work, classwork that was given extemporaneously with no prior thought, but was a message taken down on tape just as it came through. This is what makes for the freshness that is never lost even with the hundredth reading.

> Every month I read *The Letter* in its manuscript form when you return the final form to me, and then when I receive the printed copy I read it two or three times in one day, and then for at least a week or ten days after that, I read it not less than once a day and sometimes twice. By that time it has really taken root in me.[5]

The work that Joel had asked us to do and which we were eager to undertake presented us with an immense load as we wanted to continue the activities of The Infinite Way Study Center in Chicago, and I felt that the healing practice must always be the first consideration. We wished sometimes that there were at least twenty-eight hours in every day, but somehow or other all deadlines were met.

Many persons spoke about how Joel drove those who worked for him unmercifully, expecting work to be completed almost before it was begun. Few people are able to operate at such an accelerated pace. However, I never felt that he drove me, perhaps because there was a drive within that pushed and pushed. There was a sense of dedication together with the recognition that it was important that these books be published and that deadlines be met for the sake of the work which to Valborg and me was all-important.

The success of the English edition of *Practicing the Presence,* as well as that of the American edition of *The Art of Meditation,* led Harper & Brothers to inquire about printing an American edition of *Practicing the Presence.* They felt that it would be desirable, however, to amplify the book somewhat by adding a few additional chapters. This request reached Joel in Hawaii in August, 1957, at the time of the Halekou Classes. Since I was there making all the arrangements for the classes which were held in the home of Emma and Joel, I heard the news immediately and was asked to begin work at once on additional material for *Practicing the Presence.*

The final morning of the *Second Halekou Class* was a mountaintop experience, a filling of the room with a deep silence, a quietness, a sense of the sacredness of the moment, a dedication. It lasted for two hours, and Joel called it "The Experience." As I sat there listening, I knew instantly that this was to be the last chapter in *Practicing the Presence.* By the next day Ann Darling had transcribed it, and I was ready to begin work on it. Another chapter, "The Rhythm of God," a combination of work given in Portland and in New York in 1956, was also added.

Joel was delighted with these additions to *Practicing the Presence,* and upon receiving the newly enlarged manuscript he wrote to me October 16, 1957: "Just received *P.P.* Oh, what a dream. . . . 'Rhythm' is magnificent . . . 'A Vision to Behold,' out of this world. Where did it come from? What class? Well, how does one say thanks to such things?"

While I was living at Halekou Place in late 1957 and early 1958, the idea of a new book began taking shape which eventually was published as *The Art of Spiritual Healing,* embodying material collected from the tape recordings, especially some of the earlier unlisted ones available to me there at Halekou. The book was accepted by Harper for publication and released in October, 1959.

After *Practicing the Presence* was well launched, and all the classbooks except *The San Francisco Lectures* were in book form, Joel felt that there must be a book on his unfoldment on good and evil as the cause of humanhood and on the Sermon on the Mount. With that simple direction the assembling of the material began, a tremendous job because there were so many classes on these two subjects. This book, *The Thunder of Silence,* grew out of work that began with a lecture given in New York in 1956 and continued to unfold throughout all the classes in 1956, 1957, and 1958. Like all the others, it came out of an inner unfoldment—this one dealing with the first three chapters of Genesis and the Sermon on the Mount.

It is vividly clear in my mind the night in New York at the Barbizon Plaza Theater, the opening night of a public lecture, going on the platform without a single idea of what was going to come through, without any knowledge of truth to impart.

Out of my mouth came that which is the first part of *The Thunder of Silence,* all of which deals with karmic law. That is when it was revealed to me on the platform at the same time that it was revealed to those in the audience. If I had known the truth when I went on that platform, there would have been no room for that great revelation.[6] I had had to wait twenty-five years: twenty-five years of praying, twenty-five years of meditating, twenty-five years of sometimes tearing my heart out and getting no answer. And then in a moment when I had no idea at all that it was going to come, when I wasn't expecting it, it flashed into my mind like a light bulb and nearly threw me off the platform. It shook me from head to foot.

For weeks I didn't get over the shock from the intensity of the revelation that the cause of all the trouble on the face of the earth is the belief in good and evil, that nobody can stay in the Garden of Eden, of harmony and perfection, while he is accepting in his mind the belief of good and evil. But everybody can go back into Eden and be pure and live by Grace, not by the sweat of his brow, but by Grace, by the gift of God, just by giving up the belief in good and evil, just by being willing to concede that there is no good man on earth and there is no bad one.[7]

Joel was intensely interested in the progress of the work on *The Thunder of Silence.* At first it was slow because for months I was puzzled as to how the idea of good and evil as the cause of human-hood and the meaning of the Sermon on the Mount could be blended into a unified whole. Furthermore, along with the other work on *The Thunder of Silence,* for thirteen months I worked on the two chapters on "Transcending Mind" and "Unconditioned Mind" in order to clarify these principles in my own consciousness. Then, one morning in June, 1960, while in meditation, the whole pattern of the book came into sharp focus with its three divisions: I. From Darkness to Light; II. From the Unreal to the Real; III. From Law to Grace. When Joel saw the book in print, he wrote:

Halekou Place, Hawaii

Tuesday, March 7, 1961

Dear Lorraine:

Consider carefully before you answer: I believe the chapter "Unconditioned Mind" is the finest chapter in *all* Infinite Way writings. Do you feel this way—or do you have another? I keep going back over this one—again and again—always getting the same reaction—and always wondering what would come forth if some psychology professor got hold of it. I still do not "feel" the impact of the book, but I do of the chapter.

It seems that I am the parent of a baby that I pick up—put down—pick up—and wonder what kind of man I'm loosing on the world. Never had this with any other baby.

Spiritual Interpretation of Scripture was one I *knew* was unique —but I also knew that it would someday awaken a world. But this one: well, I'll just keep picking it up and laying it down —until it clicks.

Lovingly and gratefully,

Joel

The Father!!!

When the book was put on the market, the first printing was sold out in a few weeks, something that had never happened to an Infinite Way book before.

After the publication of *The Art of Spiritual Healing* Joel felt that there should be a book on advanced spiritual healing. Only a few chapters had been prepared when in 1961 Emma and Joel invited me to spend the month of December and part of January in Hawaii. I took the first four chapters that were ready to Joel to read. He liked them very much. But already something new was percolating in him, so he said, "Let's leave this for the time being and come back to it later. Now let's do a book on mysticism."

So the book on advanced spiritual healing was put aside and work begun on collecting material from the tape recordings and transcriptions on mysticism. It took eighteen months to prepare this book, which drew upon all the classwork that Joel had given on this subject, beginning specifically with *The First and Second 1958 Chicago Closed Classes,* classes almost entirely devoted to the subject of mysticism. In March of 1962 Joel enthusiastically wrote that he had discovered the title for the new book: *A Parenthesis in Eternity.* While I wrote to Joel about the progress of the book from time to time, he never gave any further instructions beyond his desire for such a book. In 1963 Valborg and I joyously wrapped up the manuscript and sent it to him, and his response is best expressed in his own words:

> Halekou Place
> Honolulu, Hawaii
> April 1, 1963

Dear Lorraine and Valborg:

I can now say my song is sung. This is what I dreamed of and did not think possible of attainment.

There are no major changes, deletions, or additions, and the finished manuscript will be just as you sent it to me. . . . I could not possibly express my feelings of thanks to both of you.

> Lovingly,
> Joel

> Kailua
> May 21, 1963

Started to read *Parenthesis* again. Am through Chapter VIII and never have read its equal anywhere. (Pardon the modesty).

Joel never realized how many different tape recordings were used to weld together a single chapter in his books or in a monthly *Letter.* For example, one of the chapters he prized most highly and considered one of his greatest, "Love Thy Neighbor,"[8] came from six different tapes, and yet he thought it had been put into print just as he had given it in class with only a few marks of punctuation inserted.

After Joel's enthusiastic response to *Parenthesis,* it occurred to me that he might like to know what tape recordings had been used in the preparation of the book. So, for the first time, I sent him an annotated copy of the manuscript of *A Parenthesis in Eternity.* This surprised him so much that shortly thereafter he made an entry in his diary to the effect that he should never have had any of his work edited. When the book was finally published, however, he recognized again the depth of his work and all his dissatisfaction melted in appreciation of the beauty of the completed book.

London
October 31, 1963

Dear Lorraine:

Life must be counted as B P and A P—Before *Parenthesis* and After *Parenthesis.* There can be no other logical division of time or mode of life.

I read it through cover to cover, and it is too broad a canvas to take in that way.

Then back to "Introduction" for two readings, then "Two Worlds" for two readings—and then "Introduction" and "Two Worlds" straight along.

These two are amazing. They set a foundation for revelation. They contain startling material, magnificently arranged. A Master hand edited these. Be grateful you could be Its servant, Its hand. . . .

As for me, my song is sung. I want no more of this world, and it has no attraction for me. I am content to stand on *Parenthesis.* Nothing can be added to it.

Every major point that has been revealed to me is in it. You have done nobly! Nature of error, name and nature of God, the natural man and man of Christ, nature of prayer, nature of communion, initiation, it is all there.

For days have done no mail. The interest is gone. Still do not know why we came to London unless it is just to get away from all who insist on coming to Hawaii. For what?

Something is turned upside down in me since *Parenthesis!* I have nothing to teach and no desire to teach. Will fill my dates up to November 19 and do not know what will follow. Will just take a day at a time. . . .

Well, this is the news today. Maybe it will be different tomorrow.

Lovingly and gratefully,

Joel

Kailua, Hawaii
February 14, 1964

Dear Lorraine and Valborg:

Yesterday and today I have been immersed in *Parenthesis*—and my heart aches with its truth, purity,and loveliness of form and expression—all three of us have done well with it.

Love,

Joel

Joel never saw *Leave Your Nets* published in book form, but at the Hilton Hotel in Chicago after the classwork in May of 1964 and before we all left for England, I sat down with Joel while he went over the manuscript. It was an enlargement of a little pamphletlike book that had been published in England years before, but this new manuscript had been much amplified.

As he read, I could see his amazement growing until finally he said to me, "What is this from?"

"The 1953 Seattle and Portland Classes."

"But this is exactly what I am teaching today!"

"Yes, I know. Your message has never changed. It has always been the same, only clad in different garments."

And this was true. In the very earliest work the principles were set forth clearly and the deep mysticism of the message revealed. Yet whenever he gave a class it was always fresh and new to Joel because it was not coming out of memory but out of consciousness.

Since Joel's demise, there have been five books published, and there are at least six more to be published. This is possible because of the way in which the books have always been prepared. At this point it should be stated, however, that while my sister and I did the organization of the books and worked out the transitional sentences, the books are essentially Joel's and the message is always his. His consciousness pervades every page.

Students were naturally carried away by the grandeur and inspiration of the message coming through him, and so they were constantly urging him to have every class printed just as it was given, never realizing how many times the very same examples were used which would hardly be appropriate in book after book. Furthermore, few persons understand that the spoken word of necessity differs from the written word. What is spoken spontaneously "off the cuff" is frequently not effective in written form. So there had to be a great deal of culling, sorting out, and arranging of material to make a unified whole and to produce some thirty books, each with its own special message. This, Joel never really understood. He did realize, however, that he was not easy to work with and in those difficult moments which were bound to arise from time to time betwen author and editor, he was quick to recognize this.

January 10, 1964

Dear Lorraine:

Have just cabled you that as usual you are right, and the March *Letter* you have done is beautiful. . . .

Sometimes I wonder why Emma and you put up with me. If I were Emma, I am sure I would kiss me good-bye and say, "Pleasant to have met you, but don't let it happen again," and I know that if I were you, I would drop me in the Chicago River with a twenty-year-old Rolls Royce tied around my neck. Why a Rolls Royce? Well at least when I am found, I want to be found in good company.

Well that's all for now.

Joel

It took courage to work with Joel, a dogged conviction that what was being done was right. Only that deep conviction and an abiding mutual respect could have continued such a relationship for so many years. And it took silence, too, proving that through silence all things can be accomplished.

Working with Joel in the capacity of editor of his writings was a rare and special privilege, but it was not without many challenges. As my spiritual guide, his word was law to me and, even though he never demanded it, I rendered to him the obedience inherent in such a relationship because I recognized the authority of his own inner experience. To combine that with the job of editor entrusted with the work of arranging his material in proper form for print, however, was like walking a tightrope. The one relationship called for a receptivity and a confidence in the teacher who had gone ahead of the student in awareness, and the other for critical appraisal of every spoken word. Yet the freshness of something flowing out of pure inspiration from a consciousness aflame with Spirit had to be maintained and was maintained, and this is the reason his writings are always new, even though a person has read them over and over. The transforming and renewing power of the Spirit, for which he was such a perfect instrument, is felt on every page.

9

Building for Eternity

A teacher affects eternity;
he can never tell where his influence stops.[1]

The great teacher defies analysis. He can neither be
defined, nor his methods dissected or described; but whoever comes into his presence feels the power of a human
spirit.[2]

During his initiation in 1946 and just as the public work in
The Infinite Way began, Joel was told that his function
would be to do what was given him to do but that he himself
would have no responsibility for doing it. That Presence
which had become his close companion would go before
him to do whatever was necessary. In the following years he
found that that promise was always kept. So, for example,
as funds were needed for publication of the writings or for
his world travels, the funds were there.

The invitations which came to lecture in New Thought
Temples, Religious Science Churches, Unity Churches, and
Metaphysical Libraries at first surprised Joel because he
knew nothing at all of their writings or teachings. The number of invitations to speak to these groups also convinced
him that such a thing could never have been accomplished

by a mere man, but that there had to be a Presence going before to bring these invitations for lectures and classwork from far and wide to his doorstep.

Classes of ten days or two weeks were necessary at first because the classes in those early days were made up of people from different teachings who knew nothing about The Infinite Way, and it took several nights for them to lose their resistance and suspicion.

The first night bristled in a classroom. . . . The students were waiting for me either to condemn Mrs. Eddy or the Board of Directors, or somebody else was out there waiting for me to say something about Unity or New Thought. They were all sitting there on the defensive. And of course I was just smiling inside. By the second night, they began to feel, "Well, he isn't doing any of those things. But I'm not going to judge too quickly." By the fourth night, however, the teaching could begin and there could be six nights of good work.[3]

In later years most of the classes were made up of persons who had read the books, and they knew before they came that there was no antagonism toward any teaching nor was there any criticism.

Joel differentiated between a closed class and a lecture. The latter was open to the general public with no requirements for admission and no admission charge. A closed class was limited to those who had read some of the writings and therefore had some knowledge, even if slight, of the principles of The Infinite Way. Furthermore, those who made themselves a part of such a class were required to be present at the opening session and attend all subsequent meetings. A class tuition was charged, chiefly for the purpose of eliminating the curiosity seekers and not primarily as a source of income. The income came abundantly through the healing practice.

Out of those who attended closed classes, there were a few who wanted to have Joel teach another class with a smaller and perhaps more selective group. That type of work began in Joel's hotel room in Seattle with a group of six who were already attending afternoon and evening sessions. For them, an informal morning session was instituted. From that original six, the class finally grew in size to where students were sitting, not only on every chair that could be squeezed into the room, but also on the floor and bed. The morning group evolved into a larger one which also had to be held in a public meeting room in order to take care of those who had been through closed classes, or who, through diligent study, were at a place where they were ready to go beyond what was given in the closed classes. Beginning in 1953 classes such as these were held for several years and were called Practitioners' Classes.

These classes were discontinued after a time because Joel discovered that nearly everybody thought himself to be ready for the advanced classes even though he had never attended one of the closed classes or studied any of the writings and, therefore, was offended if he were not admitted to the more advanced work.

When Joel first spoke in a city, the class was often small with sometimes as few as forty or fifty, but each time he returned, the enrollment increased until in his last class in Chicago at the Hilton Hotel in 1964 there were over 500 students. Not more than 250 had been expected, so the management graciously made the Grand Ballroom available for this work. His realization of the one Consciousness and of God as individual consciousness made him not only one with God but one with every person. That awareness drew unto him his own, those of his own household who could be a blessing to him and to whom he could be a blessing. It drew together out of all the world those prepared for his work.

When that work began it was with those small groups in his home where he gave the lessons on the Bible, meetings which later were transferred to his office. The students were people whom he knew, therefore it was natural to be informal and to say, "Good morning," "Good afternoon," or "Good evening," and for his listeners to respond. Joel felt that this greeting established a bond between them and created an atmosphere of oneness in which he was not a lecturer but a friend with whom they were meeting for a common purpose.

Although the audiences increased in size, his informal style of speaking remained unchanged. It was his custom to sit at a table and speak as if he were talking to one person, as indeed he was: to the

One. With larger audiences, he remained the same person who liked to talk to his friends and felt at home in talking to them, and he soon learned that the students also liked this method of carrying on the work.

There was no affectation when he spoke, none of the oratorical style, no gesticulating, none of that self-centeredness that characterizes so many speakers, who appear to be watching for the effect of every word they say, trying to determine what the audience reaction will be. Joel had a message, and he knew that he was but the mouthpiece through which that message was coming, so he spoke straight out, loud and clear with no embellishments.

He spoke very forcefully with such confidence and assurance that many persons commented on the authority they felt in his voice, and because of the sixteen years which had been devoted to the practice of the principles that had been revealed to him, he spoke with conviction. Even with all the demands made on him for teaching, he continued to maintain an active healing practice. He firmly believed that no one had the right to teach who knew only some words. Those words had to be proved by works.

> I will repeat to you what I have said to the classes since the beginning nine years ago: A person who turns aside from the healing work will not long be equipped to teach. He will not have anything to teach. I will never turn away from the healing work, no matter how big it gets.[4]

For him, teaching was a sacred trust. To him, there was only one Teacher, the divine Consciousness, to which he opened himself and which was functioning through him.

Joel never prepared a talk. Every talk came through spontaneously as it was given him. At the same time he was teaching, he himself was being taught from within, and he shared the lesson with those who were there to hear. This made a class or a lecture a deep spiritual experience because he never spoke out of yesterday's manna, out of what he already knew, unless it was coming through with renewed understanding and vigor.

For Joel, giving a lecture or class was always the most difficult of experiences. He dreaded it and never gave one from choice, but only under divine impulsion. There was always that uncertainty, that question: Would it really come through? He said to me once, "I say to the Father, 'Couldn't You tell me just a little bit ahead of time, just a minute before, that it's going to be all right?' But the Father never does, and so I just have to wait and wonder."

While there was no prepared or written lecture or class, an unbelievable amount of preparation preceded a class. Every class meant an emptying out, a dropping of what he had known before, and a turning within in the silence, waiting for an impartation. Occasionally a phrase or a sentence or even a few paragraphs would be given him which he could jot down to use as the basis for a talk, but this was an infrequent experience. Most of the time he mounted the platform with no human knowledge of what the lesson was to be, but with a conviction and realization of the Presence which had come to him in the long night hours. This Presence was always with him, although at such times It seemed to be more pronounced.

Joel realized only too well that the message he gave out was not his but God's, and that only the grace of God could bring it through. He knew that he did not have to worry about how it was given to the world and that whatever it was that was pushing it forth into his consciousness was carrying it forward. This released him from personal responsibility although he was aware of the importance of always maintaining his integrity and being a clear transparency. Nevertheless, there was enough of the human still left in him so that he had those moments of questioning, because before every class he had reached that point of nothingness in which he was suspended with no thoughts, no feelings, no reactions—just a blank. But it was into that blankness the truth always poured.

Perhaps this can best be exemplified by the account of his experience in a class in Chicago in 1956:

> There was a night in Chicago when I was so empty that
> . . . I begged those who were close to me to go down and make
> an excuse so that I would not have to go on the platform.
> . . . Nothing would come through. I was told to go down and

just meditate, and if nothing came through I would be excused.[5]

On the platform, all of a sudden the Voice inside of me said,
"Fifth Chapter of Matthew, bottom of the page."

I turned around and said, "No, it's no use. I know what is
there, and I don't understand it."

And the Voice came right back again, "Fifth Chapter of
Matthew, bottom of the page."

"Well, all right, if You insist," I said under my breath. So
I opened my little Bible and there I found, "An eye for an eye,
and a tooth for a tooth: But I say unto you that ye resist not
evil."

In that blinding flash, I caught the whole secret of the Sermon on the Mount, something I had never known in my life,
something you have never heard me teach, never heard me
expound, never heard me answer a question on because I
never knew it, and I never answer questions on anything that
I do not know by revelation.[6]

That night out of that barrenness, out of that emptiness, the
Voice poured the message that I had really longed for, for
twenty-five years: the secret of the Sermon on the Mount.[7]

At his initiation Joel had been told, *"My* consciousness is your
consciousness, and *My* consciousness is doing the work as you.
Never seek a student, but never refuse a student who is sent to you
for he is being sent to you." So never did Joel advertise for or in
any way solicit students, although usually announcements were sent
out to those who had asked for information, stating the time and
place that Joel Goldsmith would give a lecture or closed class. This
is the basis on which he operated throughout all his years.

Whenever Joel went on the platform, he not only went in a state
of emptiness, but also with a peculiar attitude toward those to whom
he was about to speak. He was not looking at persons: not looking
at male or female, young or old, rich or poor, with titles or without.
He was not looking at the clothes they were wearing or trying to find
out the amount of their education or the contents of their pocket-

books. What he was seeing was their true identity, that God constituted their being and that God was the life of every person there. He sat with no judgment, no criticism, no condemnation, no praise, no flattery. And that is what his listeners felt.

Without any knowledge of the art and techniques of teaching, Joel seemed instinctively to select the right method and to utilize various educational devices to make his subject clear. He never presented a principle without implementing it with various examples, and he applied it in such a way that everyone listening could relate it to himself and to his own experience. Speaking to people of many backgrounds and cultures, he found analogies and timely, vivid, and meaningful illustrations which they could all understand.

Many professional educators are unable to bring out their messages as clearly as this man, with no formal education in speech or methods of teaching, was able to do. He moved from simple ideas to more complex ones without effort and without losing his listeners on the way. A class progressed steadily from fundamentals with which most students were familiar to new ideas and concepts that were startling to those who had heard him many times. Even to a casual observer at a lecture, there was a sense of masterful composition in each talk, a gathering together of all pertinent ideas, new and old, into one unified whole. Every class reached a grand climax where everyone felt himself lifted to a new level of consciousness.

Many teachers of metaphysics and the spiritual way regard their function as that of imparting a knowledge of truth and they, therefore, approach the work from a purely intellectual or mental basis. Not so Joel. Far from giving students a body of knowledge on which they could rely, his aim was to take from the student every crutch on which he had ever leaned, every reliance or faith he had ever had in anything, including his unthinking, handed-down concepts of God. He recognized the dangers and pitfalls of blind faith, especially the false confidence that comes with some measure of success in this kind of work, which could easily lead to a student's believing he knew what it was all about and how healing work is accomplished.

From my background of thirty years, I will tell you this: I still do not know what it is all about or how it is done. I still do not know how God functions or why the spiritual activity is what it is. I cannot grasp it. The best I am able to do is to release myself and let it grasp me. I do not have the faintest idea of what it is or how it is that some of the great miracles we are witnessing are performed. I only know that in proportion as I am able to release myself from faith in what I think I know, in that degree, something takes place and produces effects in this outer world.[8]

The tools which he liked to call "the letter of truth," he considered important in developing the Fourth Dimensional Consciousness, but after the student had entered into that new Dimension, he could be but a witness to what things that Fourth Dimensional Consciousness does.

No, Joel did not believe in believing. He did not believe in having faith, not even having faith in the God a person had not experienced, and certainly not for anyone to have faith in him. The principles he set forth were the direct result of inner revelation and unfoldment which he had proved to be true in his years of healing work, but which he did not regard as sufficient reason for anyone else's acceptance of them. In The Infinite Way nobody is an authority; nobody has to be accepted, believed, or followed.

Just as in his days as a salesman he never sought to force anything on a customer, so in this new life of the Spirit he made no attempt to impress people, draw them to him, or cajole them with empty promises into following him. He wanted no following. He sought only to release into human consciousness the principles he had proved in actual practice, and those who were hungering for spiritual love found him ready and willing to share the spiritual wisdom his inner struggles had garnered.

Thousands of persons attended Joel Goldsmith's classes at different times, but only a few had the privilege of working directly with him in a true guru-disciple relationship. With these he spared no effort, but always stood ready to extend a helping hand as they walked that long, hard road that leads to spiritual attainment and Self-completeness, never encouraging students to lean on him but always turning them to a reliance on their own consciousness.

Students brought Joel both joy and sorrow, because in accepting the role of a teacher, he took upon himself the burden of their development. He rejoiced in a student's progress, and when one assumed responsibility for taking over some of the load of work he carried, his enthusiasm and support knew no bounds, as is evidenced in the letter he wrote to me when I first began giving lectures on The Infinite Way.

> London, England
> June 29, 1960

And now that the die is cast, I am sure that you are going to have the most wonderful experience since your rebirth. Just imagine that you are not only going to have the moments of terror before these meetings begin, but then you are going to have the joy of doing a dance right out on the street after each one of them is over. In other words, after the baby is born the mother's body feels so light, she feels like dancing—or at least, this one does!

While he was willing to go to any lengths to lend encouragement and help to a sincere student, he had no patience with pretense of any kind, especially with a student who claimed to have reached a state of consciousness he was far from having attained:

> London, England
> May 10, 1956

Dear Lorraine:

Thank you for letter and enclosure. Am glad you received the B——letter. Now I can share my misery.

I received a letter from A. A. telling me she is now a lecturer and teacher of The Infinite Way, going to travel far and wide carrying the *deep* message; sure that I will approve as I must have foreseen the event *as I know how ready* she is; that she is losing her home and family because of it—but any sacrifice for

---

The Infinite Way is a trifle—etc. etc. etc. My answer might have burned up the plane that carried it—I must inquire! So welcome, sister fellow sufferer! You don't have to be crazy to be a metaphysician—but it helps!

Love to all,

Joel

While Joel rejoiced when students carried his message out into the world, he recognized that with some of them it was either an inflated ego, a desire for personal profit, or a zeal with no genuine understanding. Since the message was such a complete departure from current teachings, even though much of the same terminology was used, it was difficult for students to empty out their old concepts. So there were few, fewer than few, who mounted the platform who had The Infinite Way in its essence and pure form. With most it was superimposed on their previous teaching, and what emerged from the union was a hodgepodge of half-truths. They clung to their old teaching, not really able to see the difference. That is the reason Joel felt that no one could grasp the significance of this message in a period of less than ten years.

Entering upon the work of spiritual development, he recognized that every student has problems of one kind or another. So a student might become fearful while going through an experience of lack or limitation, and be ashamed of his failure to show forth the fruits of the Spirit. Those who prospered too greatly to begin with might find that prosperity fostering their ego, and begin not only to enjoy it, but to believe that they themselves were responsible for it. Sometimes loneliness entered in, and sex attraction, too, might be a factor.

Each one has to work out of those problems before he comes into the fullness of a consciousness of one Presence and one Power. Those who have gone to the greatest heights are the ones who have worked through the most severe problems. Perhaps the reason is that such problems free the student from resting contentedly and smugly in material good, which would sound the death knell to spiritual progress. Joel considered it the duty of the teacher to lift the student out of such temptations.

The realization of truth in some students who have not been sufficiently purged of personal sense results in a glorification of the ego. When the teacher begins to reveal the nature of God as *I,* an insufficiently prepared student can easily misunderstand the way in which that word is used. He may believe that the teaching of *I* refers to his human selfhood, instead of understanding that the more he lives in the realization that *I* is God, the more he becomes aware of the nothingness of that personal sense of self that is always justifying, protecting, or glorifying itself.

The spiritual life begins to change the nature of the student who, because of that, may find himself in that transitional state where he is cut off from society. Doubt then creeps in, and he wonders if he is losing everything he holds dear, because he does not understand that eventually he is going to find enduring companionship with those who are his own. As long as he is completely involved in time-consuming social activities, he is not free to enjoy the companionship of those who are to become a part of his experience, or to travel as may sometimes be necessary to be in their company.

So the student, in the stage of witnessing friends, relatives, and the world fall away, sometimes becomes fearful and reaches out to anyone or anything that promises to assuage his loneliness because he cannot face being alone. But unless a student can weather that desert of aloneness, he cannot enter into the fullness of the spiritual life.

The few students who worked closely with Joel very often thought he was severe and hard on them—and he was on some. One time in Halekou I said to him, "Joel, sometimes I tremble inwardly when I am around you."

"Why, I've never been hard on you."

"No, but I guess it's because you drive me to be hard on myself." And that was it. His own inner drive which permitted no compromise communicated itself to the students.

> If they are students, be assured that I am standing over them with a whip to see that they are using that monthly *Letter,* that they are studying these writings, that they are practicing their meditation.

When students come to me and say, "I want to be your student. I want you to teach me," they are in for it. They are in for a hard time because they are either going to live up to this principle and work and put themselves into it or they are going to take themselves out of my life because I have no time for time wasting. I am working too many hours of the day myself, too many days of the week, to put up with those who think they are going to get into the kingdom of heaven on greased lightning. I know neither day nor night, Saturday nor Sunday.

I will work with students, but be assured that they will have to work with me, too.[9]

As a teacher, Joel prodded a student until that student began to have sufficient periods of inner communion; he nagged him if necessary until he could see by the student's outer life that he had in some measure attained. He demanded the same absolute honesty from the student that he himself gave because he knew that if a teacher lied to a student, he would lose his capacity to impart truth, but on the other hand if a student lied to a teacher, the student would lose his contact.

In the unpublished material which he gave me, I found the following undated paper:

The first lesson is secrecy. Why? The world must itself *note* that you are of God. It will not believe if *you* say you are. Indeed if you have to say it, it isn't so. Therefore, to attain God, first, keep secret your work, study, and effort. Do not speak of God or truth or religion unless asked, and then say very little. Keep holding back. *Let* the seeking come from the individual, and *you* speak sparingly when spoken to.

In silence make your contact with God. In silence maintain it. Since the personal "I" is the devil, use the word sparingly. Resist the temptation to think or speak of "I," "me," or "mine." Use the word God and see how it changes your life. A prophet teaches, "Learn to die while living."

Second lesson: truthfulness. To utter a falsehood sets up a sense of separation from Truth, God. There are no excuses for lying, no reasons for lying in the spiritual life. Where there is no lie in the mind or on the tongue, there is no false relationship to God or man. Under no circumstances utter a lie, and personal selfhood will be contained.

This is a rigid test of one's spiritual disciplehood. It means one's progress toward Christhood or spiritual identity. *Only* humans can lie—never the Spirit. To lie is to place *yourself* in bondage to humanhood. No one does it *to you.* No one hinders your progress. Utter no falsehoods. All relationships become of the nature of the Father and son, a spiritual brotherhood.

Continue in secrecy. Do not tell anyone that you are truthful or that you do not lie. Let him discover it in his dealings with you.

A real spiritual teacher is one who not only imparts the letter of truth but keeps the student with him long enough to raise him in consciousness to where he can spiritually understand truth, and that cannot be done in a few days. While it is possible for a person to go through a class and be illumined in a one- or two-week class, that is only because of the years of study and preparation that have gone before. The illumination comes when the student has been on the Path and has arrived at the place of no longer being concerned with the gifts, but with the Giver, of stopping the search for miracles and beginning to search for the one great Miracle.

It saddened Joel's heart to see how freely and glibly some students could talk about their love and devotion to him and how few backed up such protestations in a concrete way by action and deed. There must be a givingness on the part of both the teacher and the student. Something must flow out from the teacher to the student, but that givingness must also flow back from the student to the teacher. Without that, there is no spiritual bond, and all the talking about love and devotion will never rise above empty words.

Between a spiritual teacher and a student, there has to be a feeling of warmth, trust, confidence, joy, and friendship. These factors must be operating in a very marked degree, otherwise there is nothing left but cold intellectuality, and under those circumstances there cannot be a flow of the Spirit. Spiritual teaching generates a great sense of love, but a love of an entirely different nature from the human kind. There is nothing sensual about it, nothing of what the world interprets as personal, and yet it is both personal and individual. It is personal in that the student and teacher both feel it, yet it is on such a high level of love that it never comes down to any sense of injustice, unfairness, or anything of any nature that has no place in a spiritual teaching.

The relationship with the student is not impersonal. There is something very personal about it, personal in the sense that with every student who brings himself to my attention his life becomes important to me, his spiritual progress. I glory in every step of spiritual unfoldment that the student experiences and every bit of fruitage that comes into his life.

When students are struggling toward that spiritual goal, it is my joy to work with them, whether in person or by mail, and those who have experienced that know that there is no limit to the amount of letter-writing that I can do when the occasion warrants and when the student is able to accept the instruction, even if sometimes it comes in a very severe way. All of that to me is personal.

In the same way, when students are going through difficulties, that too becomes personal to me, and I go far out of my way to help them through those periods and to stand by with them. It is just as personal with me when they fall by the wayside, as some inevitably do. I am sure there was nothing impersonal in the relationship between Jesus Christ and his disciples and apostles. His teaching and his relationship with them were both close and personal.

The spiritual teachers whom I have met around the world feel a deep love for their students, rejoicing in those who prosper spiritually, and a deep regret for those who do not seem to have the capacity to grasp the meaning of a spiritual

way of life. That has always been the way it has been with me.
In fact, I am aware that it is often said of me that I have pets,
that I have favorites, and you may be assured of this, I have.
But the pets are always those who are devoting their lives to
this message. With them, I will share and give anything. There
is no limit.

Every time I see students anywhere trying to break through
that personal sense of self, struggling with sincerity, it is my joy
to work harder with them, not so much making pets of them
as giving them the additional time or effort that may be required at some particular point of their unfoldment.

Spiritual teaching to me is personal. It has to do with an
individual who today is a teacher working with one who today
is a student, meeting on the level of the Spirit, the Soul,
thereby forming a bond greater than any human relationship
that has ever been known. It is closer than any relationship that
exists between man and wife or parent and child. It is a deeper
relationship because it has in it none of the personal sense of
selfishness that all too often comes into those relationships of
man and wife or parent and child.

There is no sense of self in it, and the reason is that neither
the teacher nor the student can gain anything of a temporal
nature from that contact for spiritual unfoldment. Only the
Spirit and the fruits of the Spirit are received, and it isn't
something that is received so much as something that the student in turn gives or imparts to others.

This relationship is beautiful because neither teacher nor
student can personally benefit from it. It requires a greater
sacrifice than any other relationship because of the greater
demands that are made upon them through the very activity of
the Christ functioning in their consciousness.[10]

There was an even deeper kind of teaching that Joel did with a
few students, and I had the privilege of having that experience with
him. It was a teaching without words, done completely in the silence
as we sat in deep contemplation. But without a word being spoken,

there was an impartation from him to me and with it enlightenment. Joel described such teaching in these words:

> Every once in a while I find a student able to receive such teaching, and we have long periods of complete silence in which no word is spoken, and none thought, and yet the message is conveyed. That is an absolute teaching because no personal sense enters into it, either in imparting or receiving. It is accomplished completely on the spiritual plane.
>
> When you come to the Absolute, you are in the divine Consciousness, and the human sense of truth has dropped away.
>
> Truth Itself imparts Itself through the teacher-consciousness, and where the student is receptive, that teaching is received—not in the mind—but in the soul. The only way you have of knowing that he has received it is that the light is shining in his face and the fruits of the Spirit are appearing in his experience.[11]

This is the ultimate in spiritual teaching, and in doing this Joel proved himself the true mystic and the great teacher.

IO

◈ The Alchemy of the New Element

No one was more aware of the inequities and inequalities existing in the world than was Joel Goldsmith. Living in the midst of a teeming city, he saw at firsthand one of the early strikes of the International Ladies Garment Workers Union in which men and women were beaten up, seriously injured, and even killed in the name of business. He never forgot that when the steel workers in Pennsylvania struck for a wage of $1.50 an hour, the militia was called out to shoot them down. Events such as these left an indelible impression on him.

Then, too, his traveling career enabled him to see the evils existing in other countries, the sharp tensions between nations and the delicate balance that maintained an uneasy peace in the early 1900's which could so easily be upset.

These early impressions led him to wonder where God was in all this and to seek for an explanation. But it did more than that. Joel was never one to sit passively by, letting the fruit of inaction have full sway. He was a man of action, action based on very definite ideas of what was right in any given situation in terms of his frame of reference.

Thus it was that in World War I he enlisted in the Marines to fight for what he believed was freedom and democracy.

Even before the war was over, however, his disillusionment had begun. He saw the tremendous waste, the inefficiency, and the downright dishonesty of some government officials. It came very close to home because that inefficiency, waste, and dishonesty resulted in a grossly inadequate diet for the men at the Marine base where he was stationed in 1917. This so incensed Joel that he slipped away one week and went up to Washington where in the middle of the night he gained the ear of a high official in the Masonic order who was able to bring the situation to the attention of key congressmen who eventually had it corrected.

Joel was an unrelenting adversary of the Roosevelt administration. When the bill to increase the size of the Supreme Court came before Congress, which in the eyes of its opponents meant "packing" the Court, his response was immediate action. Only this time it was a different kind of action. The night before the bill was to come up for a vote, the Voice that was always there to impart Itself to him told him not to go to bed but to stay up and pray.

Throughout the hours of the night he meditated, read, meditated, and read, not praying for the defeat of the bill, but spending hours waiting for something to come through, and at four o'clock in the morning the answer came that the work had been done and he could go to bed. The following morning, newspapers came out with headlines that if the bill passed it would mean the end of freedom in the United States. The bill did not pass, and years later the editor of a chain of newspapers told how he had been awakened at four o'clock on that particular morning by a voice in his ear, saying that the bill must be stopped. He sent out word to all his newspapers to enlist public opinion against the bill, with the result that the nation was so aroused that the bill was defeated.

For a man who was a mystic, he was that strange anomaly of a man of action, too. Many people in the world sit passively by and grumble and growl. Not so Joel. When he saw something that needed to be corrected, he was right in there pitching. While in England in 1956 his good friend in Germany was in some financial difficulty, and Joel, unaware that it was not permissible to send currency out of England and thinking only of helping someone in an emergency, sent an

American bill to Germany with a letter, saying, "Here's some temporary help."

The postal authorities in England opened the letter, and an official of the British government wrote Joel that he had violated the law, that his money had been confiscated, and if he had any answer to send it to the post office department. His answer said in part, "If you have opened the letter and found the money, then you have also had the opportunity to read the letter, and you will see that I was answering a call from somebody in distress, what you might call, if you like, an act of mercy.

"Your government is founded on the Bible, on the teachings of Jesus Christ, more especially on love, mercy, and helpfulness, doing unto others as you would have others do unto you. I cannot imagine that the Parliament of England would really pass a law nullifying a law of Jesus Christ."

The postal authorities returned the money to him. Joel's faculty of persistence in the pursuit of what he considered justice had won out. How many people would only have grumbled! But with Joel it was always a matter of action.

Naturally a person who believed as firmly in and taught as zealously as did Joel the fatherhood of God and the brotherhood of man would never make any distinction between races, nationalities, or creeds. For example, some of the members of a Hebrew synagogue in California had witnessed healing and regeneration in the life of one of their congregation, so they invited Joel to address one of their meetings.

When the chairman introduced Joel to the group, she explained that she had been told that there was something missing in the teaching in this particular synagogue and she understood that Mr. Goldsmith could explain to them what it was.

Joel stood up and graciously thanked the chairman for the introduction and then began, "Yes, I would be very glad to tell you the one thing that is missing. It is the Christ." Can you imagine the look on their faces when he said that?

Then he went on, "Oh, don't let that startle you. The Christ is missing from your teaching, but don't feel bad and don't think that you are alone in that. It is also missing from the Christian teaching. They do not have the Christ either. You, as Hebrews, do not yet believe that the Christ has come, and you are waiting for the coming of the Christ or the Messiah. But our Christian friends believe the Christ was here for thirty-three years and disappeared, and they are waiting for him to come back. So they are as much without him as you are. Metaphysics forms a bridge between the Christian and Jewish teachings and explains that both are wrong because the Christ is here and now. The Christ is the activity of God or the Spirit of God in your consciousness once you have recognized It, once you have realized what Jesus Christ meant when he said, 'Before Abraham was, I am.' ''

Joel went on talking along this line for about two and a half hours, telling them about the Christ. When he had finished, one man in the congregation arose and said, "The million dollars that a great philanthropic foundation has just contributed to the Conference of Christians and Jews should have been given to you because, as wonderful a work as the Conference is doing, when its members go home from one of its meetings, the Catholics will still be Catholics, the Protestants will still be Protestants, and the Jews will still be Jews. But when we go home tonight, we will go home as the children of God."

Joel's attitude was always one of universality. It made little difference to him whether a person was a Jew or a Gentile, whether he worshiped in a mosque, a temple, a synagogue, a church, or a metaphysical center. He recognized that in any one or all of those places it is possible to know God's presence and to receive God's grace. If the Spirit of the Christ is upon him, what difference does it make whether a person belongs to an organization or not?

This mystic who believed that God was expressing as individual being, thereby making inevitable the dignity of man, was a rugged individualist. He was convinced that every man had the capacity to surmount obstacles created by his environment and heredity because when he realized his true being, he could rise above the outer circumstances of his life. He often pointed out the number of men who today are occupying positions of respect, honor, and authority who had come from the Lower East Side, the Bowery, the poorest, ugliest part of New York City, and in spite of that had become successful. His philosophy was that it is not the circumstances that dominate man, but that man has the capacity to dominate circumstances.

To Joel, the dignity of man applied to every person irrespective of race, and he had definite ideas of how the racial problem which had reached a boiling point in the sixties could be resolved:

> To those whites who are abusing the Africans in Africa and to those Africans who are retaliating, if they are students of The Infinite Way, we are saying, "Do not take up the sword, but work out this matter by peaceful means."
>
> Certainly I do not believe that there should be another Civil War in the United States, because it would be no more of a success than the first Civil War. And to send our armed forces into any part of the United States to take up weapons against other Americans, whether whites or blacks, is absolutely against every Christly principle that was revealed two thousand years ago through Jesus.
>
> Therefore I must say to the Negroes of the United States that certainly you know that we are all born equal and that there must be equality: equal justice, equal opportunities for education, equal opportunities for business expansion, employment, self-employment, equal opportunities to occupy any piece of property under the American flag. All of this must be. None of this must be done by arms, but by peaceful settlement.
>
> The Negroes are not the only minorities that we have had in this country. In Hawaii for many decades, the Orientals have been the minority, and they have been just as badly treated here as the Negro on the mainland, and today they have won equality to the extent that they comprise more than 60% of our State Legislature. Out of two Senators and two Representatives in Congress in Washington, three are Orientals and only one Caucasian. Our City Council is more than three-quarters Oriental; our schools are staffed at the very least by 50% Orientals, or more, and yet not once did they call upon the United

States Government to bring any of this about by force of arms. They won their way to this by education, culture, integrity, fidelity.

All across the mainland U. S. A., the Hebrew has been a minority, and in many places a mistreated minority, a minority not permitted in certain hotels and still not permitted in some clubs, and in many cases barred from living in certain neighborhoods. In New England this was once true of the Roman Catholics.

In no case were equality and justice enforced by arms, but in every case by education, culture, responsibility, and integrity.[1]

Joel had very definite ideas about equality in marriage. On November 18, 1959, two Infinite Way students, Ann Darling and Alec Kuys, were married at the Unity Center in New York by Rev. Sig Paulson, and after the brief ceremony, Joel gave an informal talk, setting forth his ideas on the marriage relationship:

This is the first time in my experience that I have been asked to talk on the subject of marriage. I've lived it, but this is the first time I've had an opportunity to talk about it.

In this marriage, we have one of the first experiences of students of The Infinite Way uniting in marriage and having the opportunity of showing, first of all to us and then to their world, what a human marriage can be when entered into through spiritual realization, through a spiritual relationship.

Human marriage itself, as we know it today, is not too successful, but it would be unnatural for it to be successful, as marriage is known today; because it is said that in marriage two become one, and that has been interpreted to mean that one or the other loses his identity and individuality, and the wife even loses her name.

Two becoming one does not mean the separation or the loss of individual identity or individuality, for this is an utter impossibility. An individual remains an individual, not only from birth to death, but actually long before birth until long, long after death. We never lose our individuality; we never lose our uniqueness. It is an impossibility for an individual to give up, to surrender, or to lose that which constitutes his being, and human marriage tries either to make the man or the woman submit himself or herself and surrender that which is most precious in the sight of God: one's individual expression of God being. Each of us is individual, and each of us has individual qualities, each of us has individual talents and gifts, and these are not to be surrendered in marriage. . . .

Therefore in a spiritual marriage there is not bondage but freedom, but this is not true in human marriage. It is true in spiritual marriage, where both recognize that in marrying they are setting each other free. This is the only thing I have discovered in thirty years of this work that will make possible such things as happy marriages, peaceful marriages, successful marriages: the ability to set the other free and each live his own individual life, and yet share with each other without demanding.

In human marriage a husband has certain rights and a wife has certain rights, but in a spiritual marriage this is not true. Neither husband nor wife has any rights: they have only the privilege of loving; they have only the privilege of sharing. They have the privilege of giving, but they have no right to demand anything of the other. We do not leave human experience while we hold someone in bondage to our rights.

In marriage in the human world, a husband undertakes the support of a wife. Spiritually a wife never expects this, because it would be giving up her God-given heritage of maintaining in consciousness her union with God, in which she finds her supply. When she does, the husband is free to share, without the bondage of being under the impression that he is legally compelled to do something. None of us likes to do anything under compulsion, whether legal compulsion or moral compulsion, but we all enjoy the freedom of giving. This is natural. No wife feels honored in being called upon to fulfill a duty or obligation, but every woman must feel, as every man does, the great joy of giving and sharing spontaneously, when it is permitted to be free will, an offering of the heart, not of the law court.

The return of the Prodigal to the Father's house is the mystical marriage. When an individual under the sense of separation from God becomes reunited in Spirit and finds in the mystical relationship conscious union with God, this is termed the mystical marriage. In other words, man separated from his Source is never complete.

On the other hand, when an individual finds his conscious oneness with God, he finds his oneness with all spiritual being and idea, and this includes every relationship in heaven and on earth. Therefore, marriage on the human plane is really the consummation of the mystical marriage, our conscious union with God. Without conscious union with God, no human marriage can endure, because it is not true that in union there is strength, except that in union with God there is strength. When we then, individually, man and woman, make our conscious contact with God, we have made our conscious union with our husband or wife, with our children, with our neighbors, with our nation, and with the nations of the world. There is no such thing as strength in union unless the relationship first is union with God. Then we are strengthened in our union with each other on every level of human society.

Let no one believe that a marriage is a permanent institution which has not first been experienced by both the husband and wife in their conscious union with God. Then this makes a union between them that is impossible to break. Sometimes it is said in the marriage ceremony that what God has joined together, let no man put asunder. But of course you recognize that this is impossible. What God has joined together, no man *can* put asunder. It is an indestructible relationship, that which God has cemented, that which God has united; but there is no unitedness, there is no union except in conscious union with God.

If I may say this to you from personal experience, discords

have no way of entering the home or the marriage of the couple who unite in meditation frequently. If this life of the spiritual world, of spiritual activity, has taught me anything, it is this: where we unite in meditation, a love develops. There is the love between the teacher and the student, which is indestructible. There is the love between students which is indestructible. There is the love between man and wife which is closer than any relationship imaginable. There is the relationship between parents and children which is something not understood in this world, because it is not of this world.

A marriage, then, which is not to be a marriage of this world but is to be a marriage of *My* kingdom, the spiritual kingdom, a marriage that is not to have the peace that the world can give but is to have *My* peace, must be a marriage that is not only united in Spirit, but one in which the union is maintained by constant meditation, in which we unite with God and with each other.

This is the secret of meditation. In meditation we unite with God, and in uniting with God, we find ourselves united with all mankind receptive and responsive to the spiritual urge. More so is this true in marriage. In uniting with God, especially where man and wife together unite with God, they find a union or unitedness between themselves which is indestructible, because it is much more than a personal relationship. It rises above even the good of human relationships. It dissolves all that is evil in human relationships. It dissolves all that is sensual, all that is jealous, all that is malicious, all that is demanding, and it becomes the free will gift of God to us, and the free will gift of God to each other.

There is no such thing as a question that can come into a home that cannot be solved by united meditation when each enters it, not for the purpose of gaining his will, wish, or desire, but rather of surrendering his will, wish, or desire, so that the will of God may be made evident. This is the secret, and there is no other. Human relationships on every level of life can be harmoniously maintained only, however, in the surrender of our will to God, not in the surrender of our individuality to each other.

Let us always honor and respect the individuality of the other. Let us remember that no two people have grown from childhood to maturity without developing individual traits of character, of habit, of living, and let us never believe they can surrender these just because they have entered into marriage. Therefore, even sometimes when the ways, the modes, the means of our partner are not completely that of ourselves, let us forget that. In giving them their freedom to be themselves, and as long as they "be themselves" in union with God, marriage is an indestructible relationship on earth as it is in heaven.

Along with that sense of the dignity of individual being, there was an innate contempt for unthinking mass action. Joel maintained that no *group* of individuals could create anything. It always takes a single individual. True, two or more individuals working together, each recognizing his God-given individual capacity, could draw on their infinite individual resources, and thereby would be able to succeed in a creative enterprise.

Having been brought up in New York City in the days of open immigration when anyone with five dollars in his pocket could come into the United States, he observed that these immigrants and their children were often the best students in school. After being deprived of their right to develop their individual capacities in the country from which they came, now that they lived in a free country and could attend free schools, they were intent upon bettering their lot and improving themselves. That the United States made it possible for an individual to develop his full potentiality may have been one of the reasons Joel had such an abiding love for his country.

He became angry and upset when he talked about war. One of the things that he never found possible to understand was the sending of young boys out onto the battlefields to be killed. Nevertheless, in spite of that he maintained that it was the duty of citizens to answer the call to military service, thereby rendering unto Caesar the things that are Caesar's. To refuse to fulfill that obligation was to place the responsibility upon other persons. It was his contention that if the men who made the wars had to go out to fight them, there would be no wars.

Nobody goes to war except to preserve what he believes is his human life or his human supply. The horror of it is that there are always persons willing to send their children off to be killed as long as they can stay home and be saved. The children must go off and be wounded, killed, or demented so that their elders can stay home and have abundance and preserve their lives.[2]

In World War II he was called upon by many of his patients and students who had sons and daughters in the service and asked if he would pray for the protection of their young people who were rendering military service to their country. This he agreed to do, but only on the condition that the young people themselves really wanted the help and were willing to cooperate with him. He knew that they would have to be willing to pay a price for safety and security.

There were about twenty young men who did agree to cooperate with him and among those twenty-odd there were no fatalities: no one wounded, no one taken prisoner, and not one hospitalized for any reason. All came back completely whole. Joel wrote to each one of them every week, but the responsibility they were required to assume was to write to him every week no matter where they were, no matter what the circumstances or conditions. Somehow or other they had to find a way to get at least a postal card into the mail to him.

Sending the card, however, was the smallest part of their responsibility. The most important demand that he made of them was that when they awakened in the morning they would pray first for the enemy and not for themselves, not for their allies, and not for their families back home. They would give the first fruits to God by praying for the enemy. After that he did not care for whom or for what they prayed the rest of the day, but they must follow the command of Jesus Christ to pray for their enemies.

Joel had watched the principles of The Infinite Way renewing, restoring, healing, and supplying those who turned to someone who had received enlightenment and who knew these principles. Very early in his career he began to search for the impersonal Christ and impersonal Christ-healing which would be universally available. He felt that the problems of people all over the world—war, corruption in government, inequality of opportunity, prejudice against minorities, breakdown in family life because of unhappy relationships, catastrophes, and the myriad troubles which seem prevalent everywhere—should be healed through the realization of the impersonal and omnipresent activity of the Christ.

In the early days of The Infinite Way further enlightenment on this subject came to Joel when he was living in Santa Monica. A patient telephoned him and said she had been called to Boston on some business. This occurred during World War II, and because this was a hurry-up trip she had no time to make reservations across the country, but time only to buy a ticket and be on her way. She called to ask for spiritual support because she wanted every bit of help that she could get.

A couple of days later he received a telegram which said, "Left the hotel one hour before." At that time he did not know the significance of that telegram, but later the newspapers came out with the story of the La Salle Hotel fire in Chicago in which many persons were killed. That is where she had been staying, but she had left an hour before the fire broke out.

Some weeks later Joel picked up a copy of *Life* Magazine while he was waiting to take Nadea and her mother to dinner. In it were pictures of the La Salle Hotel fire which brought the incident of the telegram back to him, and the question that was uppermost in his mind was what would have happened if there had been people in the world realizing the omnipresence of the Christ, the Christ as an ever-present activity everywhere available impersonally and universally, and if they had been realizing every day this actual consciousness of the presence of the Christ. What would have happened to those who had been lifting their thought to the Christ had they been involved in a tragedy such as this? Would they not have found that

Christ? Why should it be an impossibility to be so consciously aware of the activity of the Christ and Its presence and power that anywhere or any time, day or night, anyone who lifted his thought to the Christ should not find It there as his protection and safety and security?

It was an intriguing and fascinating thought which he was contemplating very seriously after Nadea, her mother, and he got into the car and drove in to Hollywood for dinner. He kept thinking about this and thinking that even if a person were in an airplane that was catapulting to the earth or in a submarine grounded on the ocean floor, if he had the realization of the Christ or if he reached out for It, he would find It, and It would function for him if there were those who were realizing Its omnipresence.

On the way back from dinner as they were driving along, Nadea said to him, "Look what's ahead of you, but please remember that it is the activity of the Christ." There before their eyes was an airplane falling fast with the black smoke pouring out of it. As a matter of fact, it crashed at that very moment and went right down through the roof of a house. The plane and the house were engulfed in flames.

Joel pulled the car up sharp in front of the house, and not knowing anything of a concrete or practical nature to do, he sat there praying, remembering that all that morning he had been living in this idea of the presence of the Christ. Almost as soon as he stopped his car the driver of the car in back of him jammed on the brakes, jumped out, threw himself on the lawn of the house, and crawled into the house with his nose down to the ground. A few moments later he came out with the pilot of the airplane in his arms. While testing an experimental plane, the lone pilot apparently had fainted and was unconscious at the controls as it crashed. He was inside a burning plane inside a burning house, but the man who crept along the ground, keeping his nose to the ground in the grass to avoid inhaling the smoke and flames, understood the mechanism of airplane doors and how to open them from the outside. He was an ex-Marine who had been decorated five times for doing exactly the same thing, and this was the sixth time he had successfully carried out this rescue operation. The pilot, a very important and well-known person, was taken to the hospital, survived, and in the year 1973 is still living. There is no way of proving that Joel's realization of the omnipresence of the Christ was in any way connected with this incident. To most persons, it would merely be a coincidence, and perhaps it was. Nevertheless it made a powerful impression upon Joel and added further substance to his idea of the value of the realization of the universal omnipresent nature of the Christ-activity, available to all those who reach out to It.

Joel envisioned groups of people all around the world who would dedicate themselves to specific periods of the day for the realization of the Christ in connection with world problems. There was a strong urge within him to introduce this idea on a wider scale to more persons, and on several different occasions he felt that he was ready to begin this work. In fact, as early as 1950 Joel wrote, asking me to become a part of such a group to carry on daily work to realize the activity of the Christ in world affairs. But it was not until January, 1956, that he began working with a small group of students in Hawaii along this line. Then in the classes in March of that year in New York, some twenty-five persons were invited to meet with Joel while he presented this new phase of the work to them.

He emphasized the principle of secrecy and pointed out very clearly that there would never be any personal glory attached to the work because no one would know that it was going on. Later Joel invited all those who were interested in dedicating themselves to world work to participate in it:

> Are you willing to count yourself among those dedicated and consecrated people who have risen above self-seeking and who think in terms of universality rather than personality? Are you willing to give periods of meditation every day to the dissolving of the material sense which holds the world in bondage? The Christ is hidden inside of you, but you must release that Christ into the world. Be willing to sit in the silence until you have a conscious feeling that God is on the field. Then the Christ is functioning.

168 The Spiritual Journey of JOEL S. GOLDSMITH

After you have achieved the awareness of the Christ, realize that this Christ is dissolving the errors of this world—dissolving material sense—and that that realization of the Christ is opening human consciousness to a receptivity to Truth. Just to make the statement that human consciousness is being opened to truth is a waste of time, but to have realized the Christ and then to know that this realization of the Christ is operating in human consciousness to make it receptive to Truth will be effective.

In this meditation you are not criticizing or condemning anybody; you are not judging as to whether material sense is operating in this one or in that one: You are realizing that wherever material sense raises its head, this realized Christ is dispelling it. . . . Give three periods out of every twenty-four hours to the world. This is your contribution to world freedom. Therefore, three times each day open out a way for the Spirit of the Lord God which is upon you to escape into the world.

Let your first meditation period be only for the purpose of feeling a consciousness of God's presence. When that has been achieved, that is the end of that period of meditation for the world. In your second meditation dedicated to world freedom, again achieve a consciousness of God's presence and realize that this realization of the Christ is dispelling material sense in human consciousness. Begin your third meditation once again with a realization of the Christ, and then recognize that that realization of the Christ is dispelling material sense and opening human consciousness to a receptivity to Truth.

This is your gift to the world—little enough to give for the priceless gift you have received.[3]

The world is not an aggregation of many human beings, each one living his own life separate and apart from all the others. Each one suffers in the degree that the world suffers. It is not possible to be in this world, even though we are not of it, and not know of the sufferings of humanity. As Joel said, "We are in the world, and even

though we are living in a sense of greater security and greater peace
than the world, nevertheless we do owe a debt to the world. . . . and
are trying to contribute something to the overcoming of these troubles."

This worldwide daily meditation activity was Joel's response to the
evils he saw in the world and the one way in which he felt they could
be remedied. Through the realization of the Christ, here one and
there one would be raised up who would come forth with a solution
to some problem troubling the world. It would appear in a normal
and natural way, but the impetus for that activity, for that new idea
or new leader, would come from this spiritual activity of the Christ
that was being released into the world by these silent and unknown
workers. Those who were raised up to fulfill a purpose in world
affairs would undoubtedly never know the source of the impulsion
that activated them.

The issues before the world and disturbing the world of
today—dishonesty in politics and business, ignorance in chur-
chianity, lack of morals in human relationships—these cannot
be solved by the means currently used.

No amount of exposure, punishment, or preaching will improve the thoughts or acts of men and women; no moralizing,
no promising of reward, will sway the conduct of the race.
Only as the soul of man is touched by spiritual Light will moral
values be released into expression. Only as spiritual ideals take
possession of the individual can he be the outlet for the expression of ideas of integrity. As inner illumination takes place,
outer peace and harmony are made manifest in the thoughts
and deeds of mankind.

Morality, integrity, and uprightness are not of the body or
mind, but these are qualities of the Soul and appear as the
thoughts, ideals, and ideas of men and women. The soul is
touched by divine Light in two ways: through preparation in
the individual's consciousness through centuries of development, and through the touch of one already illumined. . . .

As the illumined of every age touch the darkened senses of

man and awaken a spark, these sparks in time fan into flames
of Light, and thus work is carried forward in human consciousness until That Day, long prophesied, when the Kingdom of
Heaven shall be established on earth. In this day, peace, joy,
and prosperity will be the natural experience of everyone
through all time.[4]

Joel was not optimistic about the immediate future of the world
with all its problems, but his long-range view was optimistic. He
knew the world would have to go through some difficult times as the
evils that are now rampant in the world were being broken up.

All of this is a prelude to that glorious day when man shall no
longer live by might or by power, but by that gentle spirit of the
Christ. That Christ, which is the little pebble in the hand of David
slaying Goliath, the stone carved out of the side of the mountain
without hands, when It is realized, will reveal the powerlessness of
temporal power and the glory of the one Power of whose reign there
shall be no end.

A new world can become a universal experience only as the chains
that bind men are broken. And what are these chains that hold the
world in bondage? Is it some enemy to freedom in the form of a
ruthless dictatorship, an ideology, economic disaster, war, or the
scourge of disease? One dictatorship after another has had its day;
ideologies have come and gone; depressions have come in a kind of
recurring cycle, only to be followed by periods of great prosperity;
peace after war has been but an uneasy truce; certain diseases have
worked their havoc, and then cures for them have been found,
sometimes making way for new and more deadly diseases. All these
phases of human bondage have been overcome many times only to
be replaced by new forms.

And so it will continue until a new Element is introduced into
human consciousness which will dissolve the lust for power, the
greed, and the fear which constitute human consciousness. That new
Element may be called by many names: the Presence within realized,
the Messiah foretold of old, the Christ of whose kingdom there shall
be no end. The name is not important. What It really is, is an

absolute realization and conviction of one Power which knows no opposites and no opposition. With Its coming, "the former things are passed away," and behold all things are new.

That this new Element can be introduced into human consciousness is the vision of The Infinite Way. How it can be done is the larger, broader, wider aspect of this message and its real purpose, which was never primarily to make a few thousand persons healthier, happier, or wealthier. The vision of The Infinite Way is that, through the spiritual dedication of those who embrace the deepest principles of mystical teaching and reach the heights of the mystical consciousness, human consciousness may be emancipated from itself, that the Presence hidden within may come forth in Its splendor and glory universally.

II

🔯 A Flower Lei for the Traveler

The work of The Infinite Way continued to grow: the classes increased in size and frequency; the mail became almost burdensome to answer; and the demands for healing grew to unwieldy proportions. The movement in Consciousness was gaining momentum.

Actually, Joel felt that there was no limit to the number of calls to which he could respond in any given day. The problem, however, was that most of those calls came through the mail, and everyone who wrote expected an immediate answer. This kept him bogged down at his desk, endlessly dictating mail, or when he was traveling, endlessly writing letters by hand. Rarely did he leave his desk, either at home or on his flights around the world. But he oftentimes was at the point of quarreling with God as to why a day had only twenty-four hours and a week only seven days.

With the success of the principles that had been revealed to him and with which he himself had worked and proved over so many years, came worldwide recognition and financial prosperity. Long past were the days when he walked to his office for lack of carfare. Now he lived simply but comfortably, sparing no expense that would contribute to the ease of carrying on the work. His writings had gained acceptance in many circles and had been published by first-rate publishers both in the United States and in England. His books had been translated into Dutch, German, French, and Japanese. His was the original success story.

Few persons ever knew of the struggles that went on within, however, struggles that undoubtedly came because he knew what the perfected man was and could be and yet realized that he had not attained the fullness of what he had experienced in those inner moments of silence.

There were times when Joel got down on his knees and begged and pleaded with God. Often an overwhelming sense of failure took possession of him, the sense of missing the goal and failing to accomplish what he had been sent to do. Nothing in his outer experience could, as a rule, be pinpointed to have triggered these experiences. He was his own severest critic although he never presented that side of himself to the world. To the world he was the confident spiritual teacher who spoke out of years of demonstrated experience.

In the papers he sent me was an envelope with the inscription, "My Love Offering to God," containing the following letter to God, dated November 18, 1952, and written at a time of great outer stress and inner turmoil:

> This past night has been a continuation of nightmares. For weeks now, my soul has jumped back and forth between hope and despair, joy and anguish, doubt and confidence; but last night came the hell of the realization of separation from God. Today all ties with "this world" are broken. Today all concern for persons and events is gone. . . . All hope of good here is departed, and I look forward to the unknown with a light heart.
>
> This is the end of the road. From 1928 to 1952, I really tried —my life, my work, everything went into what I believed was a search for God and God's work. It is twenty-four years almost to the month, and it has been failure. Oh, yes, a glorious failure, not one to be ashamed of. This work is a failure only after twenty-four years of having honestly, earnestly, faithfully

lived up to the highest I knew or was capable of, twenty-four years of giving to the fight days and nights as complete a sacrifice of personal interests as has been possible. So if failure, I can at least glory in it.

There are no regrets. Since my best went into it, I cannot feel that had I done so and so it might have been different. Up to my understanding and capacity, I gave it all, and failed. So my failure is my triumph. I glory, glory, glory in a great failure, and if a failure it must be, rejoice, for it is a grand and noble failure.

I know now that when men are sad and down over their failures, somewhere they know they did not give their utmost all. I have given my utmost all, so I can joy and rejoice in my failure.

And so having nothing left to place at His feet, here it is: take my failure. It is the only perfect thing I have to offer up. Take it, Father: a beautiful, perfect failure, a bright and shining failure. It is all I have, and it is Yours.

Your son,

Joel

With the writing of that letter a great sense of peace came over Joel and with that peace this message: "Never have you understood more truly. You have failed, of that there can be no doubt, but there never was a chance in all your experience for success. You never had a chance from the beginning to make a success of this. From the beginning you were doomed to failure, and the more you realize that the closer you will come to truth."

He realized that no person of himself could succeed. Whatever success a person experiences is not his but God's. God must forever remain the actor, the do-er, the be-er. God it is that imparts and God it is that receives.

Then the words came very clearly to Joel, "You can never succeed because God is the only activity, but you can be the instrument for God's work. You can be the instrument for God's labor; you can be the instrument for God's love, but nothing more than that." So the great lesson was borne home to him that he had failed because he had believed that he had the power to succeed or to fail when all he could be was the instrument for the hand of the Divine.

Out of this night of torture and self-surrender was born a new ministry, the culmination of countless weeks of toil and sorrow which came to fruition with the conviction that he could be neither a success nor a failure. This recognition involved a complete surrender of self, the little self that is so strong in every one of us and that has to be laid upon the altar, not once but many times.

Joel had not one experience only of barrenness and desolation but periodically he felt separated from that Presence that had carried him forward step by step. Always, however, this barrenness was the prelude to deeper unfoldments and greater recognition.

It may come as a surprise, even a momentary feeling of shock and disappointment, to know that this great spiritual teacher had his moments of inner turmoil. Here was a man who had had unusual success, not only as a businessman but, in the years following his experience in 1928, he had gained worldwide recognition because of the remarkable and apparently miraculous healings for which he was the instrument and as a teacher of the spiritual way of life to whom students in all parts of the world flocked for instruction. Furthermore, the shelves of libraries and theological seminaries throughout this country and in other parts of the world are stocked with the writings of this modern mystic.

It should be a comfort to those on the Path who may feel frustrated at their apparent lack of progress and desolate during periods of temporary barrenness to realize that a person of Joel's spiritual stature, whose life was a dedication to others and who had attained such heights of consciousness, should have had such struggles.

Those inner struggles—crises, initiations—were of the greatest importance in his spiritual unfoldment. Each one lifted him to a higher atmosphere and altitude, a higher degree of awareness. That consciousness that made it possible for him to walk up and down the world as a blessing was indeed bought with a price, the price of self-abnegation and complete surrender of self. Because he knew this was the price of attainment everyone must pay and that there were few ready to pay it, rather than encouraging those who set out on the path of spiritual realization, he discouraged them. While those inner struggles tore him apart, each one served to empty him completely to make way for the new wine that was to flow forth as inspiration and an ever-increasing clarity.

By 1962 Joel had gathered around him a few students he thought would be able to present the message of The Infinite Way. These included Eileen Bowden of Victoria, B.C., Canada, Lorene McClintock of New York City, Daisy Shigemura of Honolulu, Hawaii, Virginia Stephenson of Santa Monica, California, and the author, each of whom gave an hour's talk at Joel's last class in Chicago in May, 1964.

One area in which Joel felt an overwhelming sense of failure at times was in his estimate of students to whom he had given much individual attention and who he had thought were completely dedicated and far advanced, but who later indicated that they had never caught the real message of The Infinite Way, and presented it watered down by their earlier teachings. Perhaps his weakness was that he was so happy when anyone of promise was attracted to his teaching that he sometimes mistook an ardent response for a deeper understanding than the person really possessed. He was cognizant of this inability always to evaluate correctly a student's degree of understanding, and his mistaken confidence in such students caused him sorrow and disappointment. One of his great strengths was his capacity to see beyond the human appearance to the spiritual potentiality, but many of those whose potential he recognized could not respond in full to his spiritual vision. How could he, who insisted that students should look at every person and recognize his Christhood, the *I* of individual being, accept the obvious fact that some persons were unable to recognize this in themselves?

Joel's schedule of work for 1962 included England, the Continent, and South Africa. On this trip Emma and Joel were accompanied by Daisy Shigemura, and when the work was completed, the three of them had a holiday in Italy, after which Emma returned home with Daisy, while Joel went on to South Africa. It was at the time of the

Cuban missile crisis, and he sat for some thirty-six hours meditating to break through on this problem, praying continuously.

When he reached South Africa, the human sense of exhaustion took over, and he became critically ill in Capetown, where he was hospitalized and placed in an oxygen tent. He was a very obstreperous patient and refused to cooperate with the doctor who, in spite of Joel's rebellious attitude, became a close friend during his period of illness and one with whom he shared many hours discussing political and religious subjects.

Joel had been ordered to remain quiet for a period of six weeks while he was recuperating, but he was unwilling to do this and in three days was sitting up and working at his mail, dictating letters to students far and wide, and writing down some of the thoughts that were uppermost in his mind.

Life moves in strange patterns, bringing no contentment or peace from persons or from the things of "this world." This is, of course, a stage, because prior to this we all find some measure of happiness in our friends, relatives, and things.

At this particular stage of life, everything changes, and no longer can we find satisfaction in those even closest to us, nor understanding, nor pleasure. We "feel" their emptiness of Soul. And things are of still less importance since they lose all value even when having intrinsic value.

This is a difficult period of life because it represents death to that which was life. It is the death of the earthly self. It is the end of that span which glories in attainment of any nature.

And yet the new life has not revealed itself; the glories have not disclosed themselves. The emptiness of this life is clear, but the fulfillment of the new has not appeared.

This must be what was called the outer gate where one awaits entrance into the Kingdom.

"This world" has become ashes: *My* kindgom has not revealed itself. And yet there is expectancy, maybe even hope. But if not, and if this is the way the balance of the journey is to be, so be it. Thy will be done, not mine.[1]

After he had recovered sufficiently to leave South Africa, he flew to London and then home to Hawaii.

The experience in South Africa was the beginning of his last great initiation, climaxing in the long-awaited spiritual break-through into that unapproachable area of consciousness beyond the beyond— beyond words and thoughts and beyond human comprehension. In a letter to me from Hawaii, July 22, 1963, Joel wrote:

> In London last year I was told I was to be taken to higher consciousness. . . . The South African experience was not an illness but an initiation which is not yet complete. Well, Friday afternoon I was taken violently ill and had to go to bed. Cancelled my Saturday and Sunday work. It continued 24 hours and then when at its worst the Voice spoke, and within an hour was up and at my work and dictated all day Sunday to catch up on the mail.
>
> The message was shocking, but when I checked *Thunder* [*of Silence*], it is in the chapter "Karmic Law," but not too clearly stated. Would like to add about 200 words to that chapter now.
>
> The Voice said, "There is no karmic law—there is no karmic law. This is but the carnal belief in two powers and has no existence in the divine Consciousness or the consciousness of man. It exists only the same as the belief in a flat world (before 1492) but, as one man lifted the belief of a flat world from all mankind, so will one now remove forever the belief that there is a karmic law in operation or that there is karma."
>
> Of course, I can never again be the same. Think what this means to the healing practice! There is no law of cause or effect (It told me)—this, too, is a carnal belief. Also it is not true that "as ye sow so shall ye reap." This, too, is a belief.
>
> This is beyond the Absolute.
>
> Will leave this with you.

Joel's final months here on this plane are best summed up in a letter he wrote me from Hawaii:

Sunday Jan 27–63

Dear Lorraine:

Just passing on to you a secret for your inspiration and meditation:

I do not know at what part of his ministry the Master said, "I have overcome the world"—but I know now that he overcame the world in the Garden of Gethsemane. He did not die on the Cross. He met death in Gethsemane and this was the death of his human life and in this meeting of death and mastering it, he died to human life (overcame *this* world) and entered his Christ life. On the Cross he merely surrendered his body and continued living his eternal life. In the Resurrection, he showed forth his human frame. It is possible to meet death, attain the spiritual life, and yet walk around in the human frame. It is high demonstration and is only attained by those who meet death and by Grace master it by letting go of human selfhood and consciously remain alive as spiritual life. The length of time that the human form continues depends upon the continued need for it.

In all mystical literature, it is necessary to "die" to humanhood, but it has not been explained that this death is an actual death, not a figurative one—and that the life that remains is the Christ or Buddha life, the spiritual identity *even* when the human form still remains.

At some point death comes to the human, and it is succumbed to or mastered. When mastered, death *has* occurred to the human but the spiritual life is consciously lived, even showing forth the human frame, which frame may be laid aside when the resurrected one wishes, or when it has fully served its purpose. I write not from the wisdom of man.

In this light there is a purpose in the Crucifixion. Without it, they would not have witnessed the *living* Christ but they would have thought Jesus was still Jesus and he could not have gotten his message across. Probably today, because of our greater spiritual wisdom, man *will* recognize the living Christ whenever It appears in human form and thus learn and demonstrate that Christhood may be lived on earth.

Someday you may publish this. . . . You will know when the time is ripe. It may be while I am still with you in the flesh or it may be later. Divine Grace will instruct you.

Lovingly,

Joel

In August, 1963, just a few days before I left for five weeks of work with Joel in Hawaii, he wrote the following letter:

Dear Lorraine:

I have the feeling that "green pastures are before me" but not on this plane. Neither the grace that has carried me or The Infinite Way from nowhere to here—nor the help of you, Emma, and Daisy seems to be meeting the physical situation. After the ascension, I had two weeks of living in heaven—and now hell has risen again. . . .

Grace has been the secret of my life from 1928 to date. Grace has moved me every step—some of them painful steps —but Grace was never absent. Now—I can't find my Grace, and that is what disturbs me.

I have received such a clear picture of the law not operating when under Grace, such a clear picture of the law of Moses (the human mind) and the grace of Christ (living through transcendental consciousness). . . . I witness that the "natural man" is a prisoner of the mind, locked in his own man-made rules and regulations misnamed laws—and that Grace sets him free. And I have lived so long and prospered in every way of life through Grace. . . .

Well—if the Grace that carried me from New York to Boston, to Florida, to California, to Hawaii, and around the globe is with me, all is well. If not, we shall soon learn.

Lovingly,

Joel

In 1963 classes were given in Hawaii to small groups of students. From these classes it was obvious that he was preparing the students for his withdrawal from direct contact with him. Especially is that apparent in the talk of September 30, 1963, given a few days before taking off for London:

What you have had of me, what you have experienced of me, is my consciousness of truth. You have brought yourself to me, but not physically. You have brought yourself to my consciousness. Therefore, I have been in your consciousness and you have been in my consciousness, and what we have experienced of each other is this consciousness, this spiritual companionship. If you have been receptive and responsive to what has taken place, you have benefited by having been lifted higher in consciousness. But never forget this: I, too, have benefited, because in the kingdom of God there is a union. In the kingdom of God there is a oneness. Therefore, there has been a flow of consciousness among us and between us, from me to you and from you to me. . . .

This relationship is an eternal relationship, if you will have it so. Knowing this, I will certainly have it so. Never, never will I be separated from you—from my serious students. I will never be separated from you by time or space, nor will I be separated from you by life or death, because I know that all that constitutes me in reality is consciousness. Therefore, I can hold in my consciousness "my own": those whom I desire to be with and those with whom I desire to companion. Nothing will ever separate me from the love of my serious students or from sharing with them. That is because, out of my lifetime, I have found that my greatest joy and my greatest fruitage have been from companionship with my serious students: those who love The Infinite Way, those who benefit by The Infinite Way, those who rejoice in their studies. These students have been my companions for many, many years. . . . These students have really constituted my "family," my spiritual household. For this reason, I have lived [in consciousness] with my students very often early in the morning, and very often late at night, and very often in between. Where your treasure is, that is where you are going to be, and mine has been with spiritual seekers.

Since I am consciousness, I embody in my consciousness all that belongs to me. And since in the kingdom of God there is no such thing as time or space, this all happens now and this all happens here where I am, . . . in my consciousness, not in a city or a state or a country. . . . In consciousness, we are never separated. . . .

Open your consciousness and realize this: I do not exist in time or space. The only place I can exist is in your consciousness and if you let me out of your consciousness, you have let go of me because all you can know of me is what you can embody in your consciousness, and that is not dependent on physical sense.

One's physical presence is not necessary. . . . What is necessary is the realization that we exist *as* and *in* and *of* consciousness, and in consciousness we are one. . . . That which constitutes the physical frame is only of relative importance: it is here today and sometimes gone tomorrow. There is no such thing as an eternal physical frame. Why? Because *I* am not a physical frame, nor are you. . . . So it is that *I*, functioning now through this body, will eventually discard it and function through another body because the nature of *I* is consciousness, life. . . .

Be assured of this: no one who enters my life, my consciousness, will ever be separated or apart from it—in life or in death —except those with whom I have nothing in common and whom I am willing to have dropped from me. By the same token they are more than glad to drop me from their consciousness. Have we ever received any benefit from each other except a benefit of consciousness? Is it not consciousness that has blessed us? What part of me has ever blessed you except my consciousness of truth? What part of you have I ever known except your consciousness, your love for truth? Therefore, we are one in consciousness, and one we will ever be as long as our interest is in Truth, Spirit, God, Consciousness. . . . What difference does it make where I seem to be or where you seem to be in time and space, since nothing has ever escaped out of my consciousness because God constitutes my consciousness?

October saw him again on his way to London, a place that had always held a strange fascination for him and with which he felt a deep kinship. It was from London that he wrote me the following letter November 2, 1963:

Dear Lorraine:

Parenthesis must be recognized as the book it is. And it is. It is my song of songs, and it fulfills the message of The Infinite Way. It will also lessen the public healing ministry. I see this phase of religious teaching coming to a close, and the new Way will be bringing *Parenthesis* to those seeking an expansion of consciousness which will embody their good and the purifying of human consciousness *en masse* for the new generation to be born into. The activity of just healing the sick draws to a close. This will not surprise you. *Parenthesis* ensures this.

You write of my need for special help. Yes, every day I need this. This is a critical time for me. I am grieving constantly. I am too "alone" to bear it, not physically alone but otherwise. And I grieve constantly at my lack. The vision is clear, but somewhere within is an empty space that hurts, pains, and grieves. Tears are never far from my eyes.

My spiritual universe has not externalized itself in a harmonious outer world. My outer universe is as barren as mortal mind itself except that there is a sufficiency of money. That is my only sufficiency in the outer picture—the rest is barren and sad. So I have another notch higher to go. I never dreamed it possible to be so unhappy and survive. It is all such a new experience for me.

Forgive my unloading.

Lovingly,

Joel

The emptiness that brought forth that letter once again prepared the way for new inspiration, a new message, a deeper spiritual experience, which came only three days later and about which he wrote to me from London, November 8, 1963:

All is wonderfully well.

Thursday night, November 5, it came. What the Ten Commandments were to Moses and the Sermon on the Mount to Jesus, my November 5 is to me. "Truth Veiled—Truth Unveiled—Truth Veiled Again."

Am beautifully free.

As 1963 drew to a close, he caught a vision of the impact his work for that year had made:

4:45 P.M., Dec. 31, 1963

Dear Lorraine:

This is a strange day. Sitting at the desk all day with mail, looking back into 1963 and forward into 1964 with "puzzlement."

1963 has been a year of fulfillment, probably the greatest of my life. It gave us *The Contemplative Life* and *Parenthesis*—major achievements. It gave us the work of Hawaii and England 1963 . . .

Look ahead into 1964. I see nothing before me. . . . I have no inclination to travel or give classes. And the great, really great revelation of London does not appear yet in tangible form. Last year at this time I knew an unfoldment was ahead of me. It came. This year I see nothing ahead. Great revelations do not come by the dozen—just one at a time—and this one has as yet no outer form.

So, 1964? Is there a Latin term "Quo Vadis"? . . . Where are we going? How? It is a "puzzlement" but I am a Beholder.

Hope your 1964 is a clearer picture to you.

Heartfelt greetings,

Joel

The following year several classes were held in Hawaii with a hop over to Los Angeles and San Francisco in March. Then in May Joel began what was to have been an extended lecture and class tour of the United States and Europe, stopping in Portland, Seattle, and Chicago, where at the Hilton Hotel 525 students had gathered together from all over the world to have four hours of work with him.

There was a kind of fragile quality about him although even then he was not a thin man: By Grace he had let "go of human selfhood and consciously [remained] alive as spiritual life." Most obvious was that sense of detachment, of not being here or a part of this earth any more.

A few days after the close of the Chicago class, Joel, with an entourage of about eight persons, including Emma, Daisy, and me, left for Manchester, England.

The Manchester class was a beautiful spiritual experience, as anyone who hears the tape recordings of it can recognize. Then in London came two successive Sundays of what is known as the London Studio work. The second Sunday we were in London Gertrude and Rowland Spencer, close friends who carried on the work in Manchester, came down to spend the week end with Emma and Joel. Joel was in such high spirits that day that we all laughed until we cried with the fun and clowning of the act that Joel and Rowland put on for us at our hotel.

From there we went to Mary Salt's studio on Ladbrooke Walk, a small room which held probably not more than twenty-five persons. It was here that Joel gave the moving lesson on the "Act of Commitment" which is embodied in chapters ten and eleven in the book *The Mystical I*. As Joel spoke, it seemed as if I had never experienced such a deep silence as descended upon me and upon the whole group. It was the mystical experience of the Christ omnipresent and transcendent.

The next afternoon, Monday, I went to talk with Joel and told him what a tremendous experience Sunday had been for me. Immediately he said, "Yes, what shall we do with it, Lorraine?"

"I can see it as one of the last chapters in a book."

"You are right. It must not stand alone." And then he added, "I have said it all. There is nothing left for me to say or do."

I remember how I mumbled that he had said that many times before, but strangely enough this time I knew that he really meant it. Throughout 1964, and even in 1963, he had been gradually withdrawing from the world. There were many indications that he felt his work had been completed and that he was ready to leave this experience in search of the new horizon.

From a brief conversation we had together at tea in Manchester, it was apparent from what he said that this feeling of moving into another experience was uppermost in his mind. Everything in the world seemed of little importance to him at this time. The detachment was clear and obvious.

The lesson on "The Stature of Spiritual Manhood" the evening the first session of the *London Closed Class* opened dealt with the inherent and innate capacities of man as the son of God and with the invisible nature of man's being as one with the divine Consciousness. Near the end of it he made a prophetic statement: "The outer world reflects back to us our state of consciousness, and you can begin to prove this within twenty-four or forty-eight hours in this way: I ask you to look up here at me and not look at this framework, this body, this casing, but try to look through my eyes and find *Me,* discern that which is behind my eyes. See if you cannot find something about me that is invisible, intangible."

There he was, sitting only a few feet away from me, the picture of a fulfilled person, rejoicing in the thing he loved to do most of all: impart the spiritual wisdom that was his from his first initiation. As always, he spoke with the confident assurance that the years of living this truth had given him. I looked up at him as he spoke and found myself thinking, "Why, Joel, you're saying good-by to us!"

The following evening, Tuesday, Joel met with his American publisher, Eugene Exman, who was then in London on an editorial trip for Harper. Mr. Exman told me that he and Philip Unwin of George Allen & Unwin had arranged for a dinner that evening at the Garrick Club at which they and their wives would entertain

Emma and Joel. Deciding that afternoon that he did not care to leave the hotel, Joel had Emma telephone Mr. Exman, asking that they be excused from dinner but inviting the Exmans to come to their hotel suite later.

That evening Joel talked endlessly and animatedly, spinning one yarn after another in his matchless way, each one pointing up the progress of The Infinite Way and its potentiality. Mr. Exman said that much of Joel's conversation was autobiographical "and I occasionally asked questions about his life and work to prod him on. Knowing that he probably felt tired and that it was getting late, I said several times that we should go, but he protested that we should stay longer." It was well past eleven o'clock when the Exmans left. Never had Joel been in a gayer mood or in higher spirits.

About five o'clock the next morning Emma called me to come to their suite at once. She also called Daisy Shigemura and Tom Jones of Capetown, South Africa. The three of us went into the room where Joel was lying quietly, conscious but not speaking. Because of hotel regulations, the house physician was called, and he insisted on bringing in a specialist. While the specialist examined Joel, we three went into the living room and sat there, all of us meditating. Most of the time Emma was with Joel. At 8:20 in the morning she came out and told us that Joel had made the transition.

What he had prophesied Monday evening had come to pass thirty-six hours later: the framework had become a shell, and the invisibility the omnipresent reality.

Joel never was completely free of that heart-hunger that sought a human externalization of the divine communion he experienced so frequently. Most of all, the human part of him longed to be understood. He knew that there were certain qualities about him that made him difficult to live with and to work with, but these qualities which demanded much of those associated with him were a part of him only because of his intense one-pointedness and a selfless dedication to the work which always took precedence over his comfort and even superseded his concern for those close to him. He hoped that those close to him could see beyond those qualities to what was really there.

Humanly, we are hoping to find someone who will understand us. We do not really realize that it is literally true that what we are looking for is someone to understand us in our spiritual integrity, because each one of us, no matter how villainous we may be outside, knows that inside we are angels. We are so perfect that even our mother does not appreciate us. I know that, because all my life I have been that way. I have not found too many people to agree with me, but they did not know me, they did not understand me. Inside, I am a fine fellow, and I know that all my life I have longed for someone else to see that in me.[2]

I know in my heart and soul that I am a perfect spiritual individual, a perfect 100% good human being. But I also know that there are traits and habits which operate as me which I would love to be rid of because they are less than what I am. They are superimposed upon me like the dirt or the soot that gets on the face. You know it's not your face, but until you can get to that soap and water you have to bear with it.

And so with us. I know the traits, the characteristics, the human degree of imperfection that is in me. I know it's there. I am very conscious of it. But I am conscious of it because I have something to measure it with and that is what I really am. So I would like to be rid of these other things, and I live, just as you do, for one purpose: to free myself of these so that I can live as I really am inside.

You have heard me joke a lot about how I can sing beautifully inside, only it won't come out that well. And you know I am always playing the piano on the table. That's because it is in me, and I can't bring it out. It just will not come out, but it is there. And I know it. It's beautiful, and it's perfect, and I love it, but I can't get it out. And so it is that I know myself. I know that in my heart and soul, in my innermost being, I am the most perfect individual on the face of this globe. But I am sorry that I cannot always bring it out and show it to you.[3]

He longed to be free of the human tendencies that were still left in him, but as I said to him once, none of these detracted from his greatness. He was a man who had had many of the frailties of humanhood, most of which he had completely surmounted. If a few evidences of his human origin remained, such as his impatience with stupidity, ignorance, and superstition, wherever he found them, does that make his work less great or his integrity less real? On the contrary, only greater.

It was my privilege to work with him hour after hour and day after day. With these few vestiges remaining of a life long ago forsaken, he still was a monumental character, great in his unselfedness, devoted to a mission, showing forth in his daily life an unswerving integrity. For the most part he was quick to recognize his own faults and failings. Once when he was referring to these in talking with me, I said, "I'm glad you have those few human qualities and little traits of character left because they will hold you here for a while, and I'd like to have you here as long as possible. If you were perfect, you would ascend right out of this whole experience."

Freedom from these mortal tendencies came during his great and final initiation. On June 17, 1964, no longer earthbound, the gallant happy traveler had found a new land to explore, that unknown territory that lies on the other side, and he was on his way to beyond the beyond.

It was a gallant life, brave and courageous, dedicated to selfless service, as untold numbers of persons who have been blessed and uplifted can testify. But Joel never felt he himself did any of this, as he stated so clearly and with such humility in his spiritual autobiography:

> Joel can take no credit for any of the wonderful experiences that have come to him since his spiritual regeneration in 1928, nor can he take credit for the blessings which so obviously have come to thousands of people through his activities, because Joel knows that none of this rich fruitage has come through Joel. On the other hand, the *I* that I really am, who has performed these things, utters them, does them. This *I* has no

identity and personality on which can be hung any praises, and against which no failures could be counted.

It is something strange and not to be explained that I, the author of The Infinite Way writings, have not one iota of feeling of accomplishment, but more the realization of just naturally living and being and uttering that which inevitably is Truth. I realize that at some time I must leave this human scene because there are much greater works to be done when the foundation has been laid on this plane, and I have so provided that there will be no funeral or burial so that there will be no identity left to honor or to praise, for Joel is entitled to none of these things, and *I* will live forever.

 Notes

Unless otherwise indicated, the sources below are tape recordings of Joel S. Goldsmith's lectures and classes, letters written by him to the author, conversations with him, or other unpublished material given by him to the author. Tape recordings referred to in these notes are available for purchase.

1. Beginnings: Human and Spiritual

1. *The Second 1958 Chicago Closed Class*, Reel II, Side 1.
2. From a letter to author, Honolulu, April 11, 1964.
3. *The 1959 San Diego Special Class*, Reel IV, Side 1.
4. *The 1954 Seattle Closed Class*, Reel I, Side 1.
5. *The 1952 Second Seattle Closed Class*, Reel I, Side 1.
6. *The 1957 First Halekou Closed Class*, Reel I, Side 1.
7. *The 1952 Second Seattle Closed Class*, Reel I, Side 1.
8. Unpublished notes written in October, 1957, and sent to author October 11, 1957.
9. *The Second 1953 New York Closed Class*, Reel IV, Side 1.

2. The Preparation

1. *The 1956 First Steinway Hall Practitioners' Class*, Reel I, Side 1.
2. *The 1961 London Open Class*, Reel II, Side 1.
3. *The 1954 Seattle Closed Class*, Reel III, Side 2.
4. *The 1956 Second Steinway Hall Closed Class*, Reel I, Side 2.

5. *The 1959 England Open Class,* Reel IV, Side 2.
6. *The Second 1956 Chicago Closed Class,* Reel IV, Side 2.
7. *The 1958 London Closed Class,* Reel II, Side 2.
8. *The 1958 Chicago "25" Private Class,* Reel I.
9. *The 1956 Barbizon Plaza "25" Private Class,* Reel II, Side 1.
10. *The 1954 Chicago Closed Class,* Reel II, Side 2.
11. *The 1956 Portland Closed Class,* Reel IV, Side 1.

3. Interlude

1. *The 1953 First New York Closed Class,* Reel II, Side 2.
2. Hollywood, Calif.: Joel S. Goldsmith, Publisher, 1949.
3. *The 1954 First Portland Practitioners' Class,* Reel II, Side 1.
4. *The 1954 First Portland Practitioners' Class,* Reel I, Side 1.
5. San Gabriel, Calif.: Willing Publishing Company, 1947.
6. This book was latter published by L. N. Fowler, Ltd. in London under the title of *Conscious Union with God,* and then in New York in 1962 by The Julian Press.
7. *Northwest November 7 Class.*

4. Initiation

1. From a paper sent to author, dated July 11, 1963.
2. *The 1956 New York Laurelton Hotel Closed Class,* Reel IV, Side 2.
3. Ibid.
4. *The 1951 Secqnd Portland Series,* Reel XII.
5. From a letter to author, January 27, 1958.
6. From a letter to author, April 15, 1959.
7. *The Infinite Way* (San Gabriel, Calif.: Willing Publishing Company, 1960). First published in 1947.
8. *The 1956 Barbizon Plaza "25" Private Class,* Reel II, Side 1.
9. *The 1959 England Open Class,* Reel IV, Side 2.

5. No Longer the Lone Traveler

1. From a letter to author.

6. Journeys in Time and Space—and Beyond

1. *The 1960 Chicago Open Class,* Reel IV, Side 1.
2. From private papers and notations given to author.
3. Ibid.

4. This work was incorporated in the December, 1971, monthly *Letter*.
5. This lesson became the chapter "Is God a Servant?" in *The Art of Spiritual Healing*.
6. From diary given to author.
7. From private papers given to author.
8. Ibid.
9. Material dated May 9, 1959, to June 8, 1959, from diary given to author.
10. From private papers given to author.
11. *The 1962 Mission Inn Closed Class*, Reel IV, Side 1.
12. Ibid.
13. *The 1961 London Open Class*, Reel V, Side 1.
14. *The 1960 Auckland Closed Class*, Reel II, Side 2.
15. *The 1960 Holland Closed Class*, Reel II, Side 1.
16. From a letter to Ann Darling Kuys, March 19, 1961.
17. *The 1960 Holland Closed Class*, Reel II, Side 1.

7. A Movement in Consciousness

1. From a letter to author, Hawaii, January 23, 1956.
2. Letter to Katherine Glover, January 27, 1964.
3. *The 1963 Kailua Private Class*, Reel IV, Side 1.

8. Out of Consciousness into Form

1. *The 1953 Los Angeles Practitioners' Class*, Reel II, Side 1.
2. "From the Letter to the Spirit," *Chicago Anniversary Evening, 1955.*
3. *The 1958 First Chicago Closed Class*, Reel I, Side 1.
4. Ibid.
5. From a letter to author, October 28, 1959.
6. *The 1961 Laurelton Hotel Special Class*, Reel I, Side 1.
7. *The 1956 Portland Closed Class*, Reel IV, Side 2.
8. *Practicing the Presence* (New York: Harper & Row, 1958).

9. Building for Eternity

1. Henry Brooks Adams.
2. *Conclusions and Recommendations of the American Historical Association Commission on the Social Studies* (New York: Charles Scribner's Sons, 1934), p. 84.
3. *The 1958 Chicago "25" Private Class*, Reel I, Side 2.

4. *The 1956 First Barbizon Plaza "25" Private Class,* Reel II, Side 2.
5. *The 1961 Laurelton Hotel Special Class,* Reel I, Side 1.
6. *The 1956 Portland Closed Class,* Reel IV, Side 2.
7. *The 1961 Laurelton Hotel Special Class,* Reel I, Side 1.
8. *The 1961 Waikiki Infinite Way Center,* Reel I, Side 1.
9. *The 1960 Perth Closed Class,* Reel III, Side 2.
10. *The 1957 Chicago Open Class,* Reel I, Side 1.
11. Ibid.

10. The Alchemy of the New Element

1. From a letter to Katherine Glover, January 4, 1964.
2. *The 1960 Maui Open Class,* Reel IV, Side 2.
3. *The Infinite Way Letters of 1959* (London: L. N. Fowler, Ltd., 1960), pp. 141–143.
4. Written aboard the *S. S. Lurline,* March 27, 1951, 12:00 M. From private papers given to author.

11. A Flower Lei for the Traveler

1. From a paper written in Capetown, South Africa, November 18, 1962, and sent to author from there.
2. *The 1962 Princess Kaiulani Open Class,* Reel V, Side 1.
3. *The 1959 New York "25" Private Class,* Reel I, Side 2.

74 75 76 77 10 9 8 7 6 5 4 3 2